Seek Forgiveness & Be Free

LIBERATION FROM KARMIC BONDAGE

SIRSHREE

SEEK FORGIVENESS & BE FREE
Liberation from Karmic Bondage
By Sirshree Tejparkhi

Copyright © Tejgyan Global Foundation
All Rights Reserved 2016

Tejgyan Global Foundation is a charitable organization
with its headquarters in Pune, India.

ISBN : 978-81-8415-587-7

Published by WOW Publishings Pvt. Ltd., India

First edition published in November 2016

Third reprint in February 2025

'Printed and bound by Trinity Academy For Corporate Training Ltd, Pune

---

Copyright and publishing rights are vested exclusively with WOW Publishings Pvt. Ltd. This book is sold subject to the condition that it shall not by way of trade or otherwise, be lent, resold, hired out, or otherwise circulated without the publisher's prior written consent in any form of binding or cover other than that in which it is published and without a similar condition including this condition being imposed on the subsequent purchaser and without limiting the rights under copyright reserved above, no part of this publication may be reproduced, stored in or introduced into a retrieval system, or transmitted, in any form, or by any means, electronic, mechanical, photocopying, recording or otherwise, without the prior written permission of both the copyright owner and the above-mentioned publisher of this book. Any person who does any unauthorized act in relation to this publication may be liable to criminal prosecution and civil claims for damages.

Although the author and publisher have made every effort to ensure accuracy of content in this book, they hereby disclaim any liability to any party for any loss, damage, or disruption caused by errors or omissions, resulting from negligence, accident, or any other cause. Readers are advised to take full responsibility to exercise discretion in understanding and applying the content of this book.

*To those seekers of true liberation
who are not only cleansing themselves
of their own karmic bondage
but who also dedicated themselves to
liberating humanity from karmic bondage
thereby raising mass consciousness.*

Contents

Preface

Section I   Introduction To Karmic Bondage

one	03
two	07
three	12
four	19
five	26
six	31
seven	36
eight	43
nine	51
ten	57

Section II Causes of Karmic Bondage

eleven 63

twelve 67

thirteen 71

fourteen 79

fifteen 87

sixteen 93

seventeen 100

Section III Clearing Deeper Impressions

eighteen 109

nineteen 116

twenty 122

Section IV Forgiveness for Ultimate Liberation

twenty-one 134

twenty-two 134

twenty-three 138

twenty-four 143

twenty-five 147

twenty-six 154

twenty-seven 159

Appendices

Preface

There was a prison in which several inmates were serving their sentences. All of them were assigned rigorous jobs. Being in prison was a struggle, but they lived for the day that they would be released from their ordeal. They counted each day as it went by, though there were no calendars or clocks. To keep track of the days, many inmates drew lines on the wall with pieces of charcoal.

It was announced that a special celebration was coming up. The inmates knew that on special occasions, the authorities released a few inmates on grounds of good behavior. They were excited and each of them hoped for his name to be included on the to-be-released list. The celebration finally arrived and the inmates gathered in the courtyard to wait for the announcements.

The warden came out and the inmates held their breath. He said, "I see that most of you have drawn lines on the walls to keep count of your days here? The number of lines each of you have drawn is the number of weeks that you have to stay further in jail."

A shroud of gloom descended over them. Almost eighty percent of the inmates had drawn lines on the walls. These lines became chains of bondage for them. The other twenty percent were happy because they had either drawn no lines or very few.

Those who had drawn many lines were in deep despair. They thought, "I drew these lines to know the date I would be free. How would I know that one day they would turn into chains of bondage? If only someone had informed *me about this when I arrived! If I had known, I would have been free like these others.*

This is our own story. We are the prisoners who keep drawing lines knowingly or unknowingly on the wall of life.

We see caged birds and think, "Poor birds! They have wings but they cannot fly." We are no different. We too are tied down within the cage of our karma. We draw lines through our mental and physical actions, and then get trapped in the mesh.

Birds are helpless, they can't break their cages. But we can break our bondages because it is we who have unknowingly caged ourselves. Despite this, we never take any effort to break free. We aren't sensitive enough to know that we are bound, or we don't know the way to freedom.

If we want to break free from our karmic bondages and the resulting misery, we need to understand the mystery of these lines. What are they? How are they formed? How do they harm us? How do we eliminate them? We need to seek out answers to these questions.

Drawing karmic lines on the screen of life is a sign of lowered awareness and ignorance. But erasing them is an art which is less known or even practiced. If you learn this art, your life will be like those prisoners who were free even though they were imprisoned, or who were likely to be freed soon. Unless we become aware of and eliminate the karmic lines we have drawn, and stop drawing new ones, we continue to lead a life of bondage.

This book is an edited compilation of a series of conversations between seekers of Truth and Sirshree. It elaborates the laws of karma and the spiritual practice for liberation from karmic bondage in a simple and lucid way. Using examples from daily life, the book shows the way to freedom from karmic lines that block your physical vitality, mental health, social harmony, financial prosperity and spiritual wellbeing. It also helps you free yourself from karmic lines that are deeply ingrained in your subconscious mind; the core beliefs which are entangling you in bondage again and again.

These conversations have been divided into sections. As you read through the conversations in sequence, the art of freeing yourself from the prison of karmic lines will unfold before you.

The exercises explained in these conversations are simple and easy to practice in your day-to-day life. As you practice them, you'll find that life becomes light and easy. Relationships improve, money blocks and hurdles in your success begin to dissolve, and most importantly, you begin to delight in a newfound peace and bliss.

SECTION I

Introduction to Karmic Bondage

one

Seekers who come from diverse backgrounds have gathered in a series of discussion sessions with Sirshree to share their life situations and gain clarity. Three designated seekers A, B and C converse with Sirshree. The reader is encouraged to read these conversations sequentially, so as to benefit from the systematic unraveling of understanding.

Seeker A: My spouse always points fingers at me. Whatever I do, I am blamed. Most of the time, I try to control my anger but sometimes I'm not able. I just burst out on my spouse and I also look for ways to run away from it. I'm sick of this happening and I realize our household harmony is at stake. How can I solve this problem?

Sirshree: Are you aware of the snakes and ladders' game?

Seeker A: Vaguely. I played it once. But how is that related to this problem?

Sirshree: It is related. We will get to it. What about others in the room? Has anyone here played it anytime in their childhood?

Seeker B: Yes, Sirshree.

Sirshree: Can you please explain the details of the game?

Seeker B: Yes, two players play this game. The idea is to take turns progressing on tiles sequenced 1 to 100 by rolling dice. On the path, there are snakes that bring you down and ladders that take you up. You might land on a neutral tile, a snake tile or a ladder tile. From start to finish, players wonder: Who climbs up? Who falls down? Who is the first one to cross the last tile?

Sirshree: Excellent! Life is similar. People plan their next moves, conspire against others, try to push others down, they fall down, get up, and try to beat the competition. Sometimes they win, sometimes they lose, sometimes they pray for their wellbeing and sometimes they pray for others' misfortune, and so on.

Seeker A: Do you mean to say that I'm playing this game with my spouse? Are you saying that I am treating my spouse as an opponent who tries to put me down and reacting by trying to do the same?

Sirshree: Well said. You are on the right track.

Seeker A: When my spouse puts me down, I feel like the snake is pulling me down. But when I put my spouse down, I feel like I'm climbing the ladder.

Sirshree: When things happen as you want them to, you happily take the credit for your accomplishment. You feel like you have climbed the ladder of success. However, when things go wrong – like when you are blamed by your spouse, you grieve and feel as if the snakes have pulled you down. In an attempt to regain your position, you become angry and try to put the blame on someone else.

Seeker B: But how do we solve the problem? This game of snakes and ladders will go on forever. Sometimes one person will win and sometimes the other.

Sirshree: What if you're gifted a magic wand that turns the snakes in your life into ladders of growth? Wouldn't your life be smooth and easy?

Seeker C: Aha! I never thought that snakes could be turned into ladders. Life would be really smooth if everything was a ladder. But how can someone win without making the other person lose? Is it possible that both participants win?

Sirshree: If you understand what exactly goes on in the tapestry of life, whether you encounter a snake or a ladder, you always win. Those who master this wonderful art are able to sail through life easily, happily and successfully. No snake can pull them down because they are all turned into ladders.

Seeker A: Can you teach us how to do this?

Sirshree: Some people confuse snakes for ladders and ladders for snakes out of ignorance. The first step is learning to discern the snakes from the ladders. It's also good to understand the board on which this whole game is being played out. So, what is common between the snakes and ladders? What attributes do they share?

Seeker B: Ultimately, both are lines. Snakes are the wavy lines that take you down and ladders are the vertical lines that take you up – and both share the same board.

Sirshree: Excellent! You need to understand what these lines are that lead to your rise or fall. In fact these lines have turned your life into a game of joy and sorrow, hope and despair. The board signifies life itself – the existential experience of Consciousness. Every time you entertain impure and negative feelings for someone, a karmic line gets drawn on the board of pure Consciousness, linking the two of you in a karmic bondage. This is a snake that brings down your level of consciousness. The board gets tainted with these impressions. When you hold thoughts of prayer or blessings of forgiveness for others, a ladder is drawn and your level of consciousness goes up.

Seeker C: Do these lines signify *Prarabdha Karma* as I have read in the spiritual scriptures?

Sirshree: Yes. However, with the passage of time and with repeated use, many ancient words have lost their significance. As a result, people listen to them mechanically and there isn't any radical change within. Now, these concepts are brought forth using a new terminology so that people listen to them with awareness, contemplate on them, and then make them part of their life.

two

Seeker A: What are these karmic lines?

Sirshree: Suppose you comment angrily to a colleague in your office, "You're always late to the office. When are you going to learn to be on time?" By speaking to him rudely you bind yourself to him through a karmic line. Holding onto negative emotions causes blocks in energy pathways within the body-mind mechanism. We unknowingly place an order for even more resentment that rebounds back on us, multiplied many times over. The converse is true for positive thoughts as well.

Seeker B: So every time I say or do something negative to someone, I am bound by a line of bondage?

Sirshree: Not just saying or doing, even just thinking or feeling. People believe that karma happens only as speech or external actions. But the truth is different. Every thought and feeling is karma. Speech and actions are only the external manifestations of your thoughts and feelings. So the real karma happens within the mind. Your thoughts and feelings create lines of bondage. Hatred, guilt, anger, ego, and jealousy all create lines of bondage.

In fact, when you feel resistance in a situation, your feelings serve as seeds to create lines of bondage and shape your future. As a result, a series of events are orchestrated in your future. If you react to those events unconsciously, you create even more bondage and the cycle goes on forever.

Seeker C: I always thought that feelings and thoughts are my private property, and I am free to feel and think the way I want. I am very upfront in my reactions. When someone doesn't act like I think they should, I immediately call them out without thinking about how it is perceived. But now I realize that more than how it gets perceived, what is more important are the lines of bondage created within me through the way I think and feel about them. But what if someone hurts me, will that also create a line of bondage?

Sirshree: If the other person is saying it hatefully, it creates a line of bondage within him. But let's talk about you. If you are hurt by someone's words or behavior then that hurt creates a line of bondage within you. A lot of times, you suppress your feelings instead of letting them out. You curse your fortune. You seethe within and grumble mentally. This creates more lines of bondage, which can create complications within and cause physical ailments too.

Seeker C: Oh! How can the snakes – the negative lines of bondage – make me sick?

Sirshree: Some people are obese, they don't get overweight overnight; it's a gradual process. Only after they are diagnosed with heart disease, high blood pressure, or diabetes do they realize they have a problem. The same is true with mental lines of bondage. As long as they are frail lines they are ineffective. Gradually, they form bundles and gain strength. Then their impact becomes noticeable and we begin to become aware of them at the physical plane. Better to be aware of them when they are frail lines! For that, you need to be constantly aware of your intention, feelings, self-talk and reactions.

Seeker A: Yes, I agree completely. I have noticed that I get headaches quite often, usually on the days when I hate or argue with my spouse a lot. Do you mean to say that: As we sow, so shall we reap?

Sirshree: Culturally, we've been taught since childhood to see no evil, speak no evil, and hear no evil. We have been taught that we reap whatever we sow. All religious tenets guide us to avoid malevolent deeds and encourage us to perform virtuous ones. In short, we have been taught to keep distance from all forms of evil.

We have never been taught that the feelings and self-talk that goes on in our minds are the real deeds. You might behave nobly while having wicked intentions or act unpleasantly while having the best of intentions. It is the intentions and feelings that we entertain within that produce results.

Seeker B: Can you please explain how intention, feelings and self-talk create karmic lines?

Sirshree: The intention behind your action, not the external action, determines whether your karmic lines are good or bad, thick or thin. Let's understand this with an example.

A hermit was sitting under a tree and meditating. He heard rustling behind the tree and saw that a rabbit was hiding there. A while later, a hunter came by and asked, "Did you see a rabbit coming this way?" The hermit said "No," and the hunter went away. A person who watched all this from a distance went up to the hermit and asked, "You are a hermit seeking spiritual progress. Why did you lie?" The hermit answered, "A lie for the sake of saving someone's life is not a lie."

Even though the action itself seemed negative, the intention behind it was pure and positive. The hermit wanted to save the rabbit so this action does not result in a negative karmic line.

Imagine an elderly man comes to you seeking donations. You give him some money but internally, you grumble, "These people don't have any sense of time. They don't value others' priorities. Whenever they feel like it, they just come and ask for donations." Outwardly, your action is positive but the intention and your self-talk is negative. In such a case, a negative karmic line is formed.

Seeker A: I tend to put people down in my mind, but I now realize that creates a line of bondage.

Sirshree: (laughs) Yes, it does! These lines of bondage are so subtle that we are totally unaware of them. This happens when we get caught up in the daily happenings of life. We tend to go to war with the world around us and torment ourselves.

Seeker B: Please tell us more about the impact that lines of bondage have on us.

Sirshree: Lines of bondage impact all spheres of life. Mental illnesses like hatred, jealousy and guilt invite physical diseases. When we can't let go of the events of the past or the bitter words spoken by someone and forgive them, we suffer.

Lines of bondage affect us to such an extent that we lose our inner strength and get trapped in a vicious cycle of karmic lines which create more karmic lines. Victimized, we behave against our own best interests. People get hurt by our behavior and it creates disharmony in our relationships.

In drawing negative lines, we actually resist the flow of life through our bodies. Negative, hurtful memories, bitterness, and ill-will choke the free flow of life within us. This creates challenging circumstances, limitations and sorrow. We aren't open to the abundance of life and may even face money problems due to this lack.

Serious truth seekers can't persevere through their spiritual practice properly, as karmic lines distract their attention. In order to be immersed in the spiritual practice, it is essential to first cleanse and lighten the mind.

Seeker C: Oh my God! How can I cleanse these lines and how do I know when I've cleansed them?

Sirshree: There is nothing to worry about. You just need to be aware. When you understand how karmic lines are formed and when they grab your attention, it becomes easier to cleanse them.

When the lines of bondage are erased, you feel as if something different has happened. As your mind lightens you feel as if the entire atmosphere has become light, open and cheerful. You become free of diseases and mental habits and swiftly tread on the path of liberation. You experience an unimaginable joy and peace. But first you need to erase all karmic lines.

The most important and significant aspect of the science of karmic lines is that *old lines can be erased and new lines can be stopped from appearing. Complete freedom from karmic bondage is possible – this is liberation or Moksha.*

three

Seeker B: I can see that I have created lot of karmic lines by being angry and frustrated with some people. What should I do now to erase them?

Sirshree: For that you will have to first understand three mantras which act like magical dice that make you win with every move you make. It eliminates your karmic lines and pushes you towards progress. It's like you turn every snake into a ladder of progress with this dice. When you use these powerful mantras, your life will undergo a joyous, happy and positive transformation. Your karmic lines will get wiped away and you will open up and blossom in life to experience a state of freedom.

Seeker C: Wonderful! I am curious to know about these magical mantras. What are they?

Sirshree: The magical mantras are – Accept, Forgive and Let-go. You might have heard about the story of Alibaba from the Arabian Nights in your childhood. Alibaba used the magical phrase "Open Sesame" and the treasure den opened for him. "Accept", "Forgive" and "Let-go" are the magical mantras which will open the treasure trove of happiness, bliss and peace for you.

Seeker B: Please tell us more.

Sirshree: Let's start with "Accept." But before that, explain the situations in your everyday life where you resist.

Seeker B: Generally, I grumble when I leave home late and get caught up in a traffic jam, my boss assigns me too much work when I had promised to return home early, and my subordinates are not cooperative.

Seeker A: When I am not able to accept people, situations and incidents, I constantly grumble, "My spouse reacted this way. My family keeps demanding something from me. My mother-in-law ignores me. My kids are so naughty. My neighbors are not nice. And, so on."

Seeker C: I grumble when hawkers sell at exorbitant prices, my health doesn't support me, and people don't value me.

Sirshree: The more you complain and resist a situation, the more karmic lines you draw. But when you understand the science of karmic lines and become aware of them, you realize that troubles and difficulties are nothing but the parcels sent to you by nature as a result of the liabilities incurred through your karma. You have to repay the debt you owe and then whole heartedly accept the situation.

If you gracefully accept all your parcels with a feeling of gratitude, you will instantly become free from bondage. Gradually, you will settle your karmic account with nature and gain freedom from the vicious cycle of give and take. You will then move towards liberation.

Seeker A: I now understand that when I go tit for tat and give back to my spouse, I am actually drawing new karmic lines and creating bondage for myself. But at the time, I just can't control my anger.

Sirshree: Whenever you receive a parcel that brings you negative feelings like anger, disappointment, hopelessness, sorrow, worry, fear, or guilt, repeat the following:

- This negative feeling is temporary. It will not last forever. It will remain for some time and then go away.
- This feeling is not associated with me. It is associated with my body and mind, but I am not my body or mind. I am completely free from this feeling.
- This was something which was due to me and I received it today. Now my karmic account is settled.

As you remind yourself of these three truths, you can settle into the feeling of acceptance. This will instantly rid you of sorrow and also wipe away your karmic lines.

Let's understand how you can learn acceptance in and through all situations in your life:

Gautami, an old and pious Brahmin woman, lived in a dense jungle with her son. One day, her son accidentally stepped on a small poisonous snake and the snake bit him. The poison killed the boy instantly. When people went hunting for his body, they found the snake resting nearby. Along with the dead body, they dragged the snake by a rope to Gautami. She grieved over the death of her son and appeared to accept it.

People asked her, "Do you want us to kill the serpent that murdered your son?"

She replied, "Don't do that. The snake may also be someone's son. If you kill it, its mother will grieve over its death just like me."

People told her, "But the snake is poisonous and it killed your son!"

Gautami replied, "It's not the snake's fault that it is poisonous. Nature has made it that way. It simply defended itself using its natural instinct. You can't blame it for its behavior."

Seeker A: The story teaches us how Gautami viewed the entire scene impartially, without bias and accepted it. We should do the same.

Sirshree: Good! Let's talk about "Forgive" now. Imagine that a relative has sent you a letter accusing you of insulting him and having no manners. How will you feel after reading the letter?

Seeker C: Most probably, I will feel sad and angry. I will plan to scream at him and make him realize that by accusing me he has invited trouble for himself.

Sirshree: By doing this, you will start drawing karmic lines with him and get bound by them.

Seeker C: Yes? I didn't realize that.

Sirshree: Suppose at the end of the letter he writes, "I know you are not a bad person. You have several good qualities as well. But I am angry with you. So, I am venting my frustration through this letter. I'm sorry. Please forgive me." Now what is your reaction?

Seeker C: I will feel a bit relieved and stop my mental commentary.

Sirshree: A moment ago you felt hurt, however the last few words have unexpectedly soothed your wound. Thus, you immediately stopped drawing karmic lines.

It's not that the wound healed immediately. But as soon as you read "Forgive me," you stopped forming karmic lines. The lines that you already created became thin and faint.

Seeker C: Wow! It seems magical.

Sirshree: Yes, indeed! This is the magic of forgiveness. You are aware of the science of karmic lines and you will not only forgive the other person but also seek forgiveness from him, at least mentally, for the karmic lines you have created. You know that the letter is your parcel deposited with nature and your relative is merely the medium of delivery. By grumbling you create further bondage. Thus, you will seek forgiveness for both of you.

Seeker A: So, when my spouse points fingers at me, by reacting I am creating further karmic bondage for myself. Instead, I should accept the situation, consider it my parcel sent by nature, and seek forgiveness for both of us.

Sirshree: Very well understood! Let's move on to the third magic mantra. What happens when a stream of water is blocked?

Seeker B: I know that free flowing water always remains clean. If it stops flowing, it starts stagnating; moss starts forming on it, dirt starts accumulating, and the water becomes unhealthy.

Sirshree: True! The same applies for the flow of thoughts as well. If something gets stuck in the flow of your thoughts, it disturbs the entire stream of your life.

Seeker C: Do you mean to say that the grudges which I hold against people are blocked thoughts?

Sirshree: Yes, they are. When you resist people and situations in your life, you create blocks in your thoughts. Karmic lines created due to such blocks deliver parcels in the form of bad feelings, physical and mental diseases, and bitterness in relationship.

Seeker A: My God! I resist so many people and situations in my life. I hold grudges against my spouse and don't lose any opportunity to get even. No wonder I am losing harmony at home.

Seeker B: I compete with my subordinates and am always in search of opportunities to show my boss that I am better than others. This causes nothing but anxiety and stress.

Seeker C: I always find ways to blame the people around me for being cheaters. I don't trust anyone. I experience bitterness in my relationships. Now I understand that I am creating blocks in my own thoughts due to this way of thinking.

Sirshree: As you use the third magic mantra "Let-go," along with acceptance and forgiveness, you realize that whatever was blocked inside you is immediately released. You feel as if everything is easier and crystal clear. You feel relieved and experience freedom. You feel light and like you are swiftly treading on your path.

Whenever such negative thoughts occur to you, you can safeguard yourself by using the three magical mantras – Accept, Forgive and Let-go. First accept them. Seek forgiveness for both the sender of the parcel and yourself. Then let go of the thoughts and associated feelings. Don't keep harping on them again and again. By repeating them, you hold on to them. The more you focus on them, the longer they remain in your life. Accept everything, forgive and seek forgiveness instantly and finally let go; let it flow away.

Seeker A: I want to experience that. I will make these mantras part of my life and use them regularly. I will have loving relationship with everyone.

Seeker B: I will also absorb them into my life to experience harmony at work.

Seeker C: Using these three magical mantras I will lead a life, free from complaints and full of happiness and trust.

Sirshree: Good! This will ensure that no new karmic lines are formed in your life; the older karmic lines will gradually subside and will finally get erased. The spiritual practice associated with these three mantras is so powerful that you will be amazed by the results. It will solve all the problems in your life and you will start swimming in the ocean of happiness.

All the great saints like saint Kabir, Lord Buddha, and Jesus Christ have preached the importance of forgiving and not accumulating ill feelings for others. Many hear these teachings from childhood but can't practice them because they don't have complete understanding of the forgiveness practice. Further, they don't realize its importance and necessity. Once you understand the depth of this practice, you will give it priority in your life.

Seeker A: Thank you so much for this guidance.

four

Seeker A: Sirshree, as you suggested, I forgave my husband.

Sirshree: What did you do?

Seeker A: I said, "I am sorry" to him.

Sirshree: Ideally, we are supposed to say "I am sorry" or "Please forgive me" sincerely from the heart. But it has become so mechanical that we don't care to be truly sincere. We say sorry so fleetingly that it neither carries any genuine feeling nor does it touch anyone's heart.

Seeker B: True! Many a time I genuinely don't feel sorry, I say it out of habit.

Sirshree: Can you give a few examples?

Seeker B: When I accidentally bump into someone, I say "I am sorry" and quickly move on. When I reach the office late, I apologize to my boss and quickly get on with my work. Even when I overtake someone while driving, I apologize.

Seeker A: When my son is talking to me, I am engrossed in something else and I do not follow what he says. At that time, I say "I am sorry" so that he can repeat it.

Seeker C: When I can't grasp what someone is telling me, I say sorry as if I offended someone.

Sirshree: Good examples! In reality, seeking forgiveness is not the superficial exchange of words "I am sorry." It's a genuine apologetic feeling from within. The spiritual practice of forgiveness is very deep and has a vast dimension to it.

Seeker B: Could you please explain how to practice forgiveness in its truest sense?

Sirshree: When you forgive or seek forgiveness from the bottom of your heart with full awareness, you practice true forgiveness. You may seek sincere forgiveness mentally too, without actually speaking to the person. If you do it mentally, you may actually get the courage to speak up. We have already discussed the three mantras – Accept, Forgive and Let-go. Let's revise this three-step spiritual practice.

In the first step, you accept the incident that has happened. You are not ignoring it; you are accepting your emotions related to the incident. In the second step, you become aware about the karmic lines formed during the incident; you forgive or seek forgiveness from the people involved in the incident. You do this from the bottom of your heart. Finally, in the third step, you let go of the thoughts and feelings associated with the incident from your mind. In short, you don't repeatedly think or grumble about the incident. If you need to reach out to someone, you can. But the idea is to truly let go of the incident one way or the other.

Seeker C: I understand that I should practice forgiveness when I commit a mistake. I did something that I shouldn't have. And so I have formed a karmic line. As a result, I have tied myself in karmic bondage. I will have to suffer the consequences sooner or later. So, I will immediately use this spiritual practice. But I don't understand why I should practice it when it's someone else's mistake?

Sirshree: Whether or not it is your mistake, did you grumble about it mentally? If you thought of the other person as a separate individual, a separate body-mind, then you have not grown spiritually. When you seek forgiveness by reminding yourself of your true nature, Consciousness becomes pure again. As you grow spiritually, you begin to understand that the biggest obstacle to spiritual growth is assuming that you are your body – separate from the one existential experience of Consciousness.

Identification with the body is the main obstacle for Self-realization. When you believe that "Whatever is inside the skin is me and everything else is 'others'" you are not honoring the truth of who you truly are. Your true essence is Consciousness. The person whom you consider as 'other' is also essentially the same Consciousness.

Allow yourself to be in a meditative state and then think of the relationship in question. Seek forgiveness for considering yourself and the other to be individuals or separate bodies.

Whether you felt hurt by someone or you hurt someone, whether you are at fault or someone else is at fault – you are carrying an imprint that only reinforces the belief that 'you' and 'I' are separate individuals housed in bodies. You can use every relationship to reinforce who you truly are by seeking forgiveness for believing in this separation. This is the spiritual practice of forgiveness for liberation.

Even if someone else is at fault, you are forgetting that it is your own parcel that nature has sent to you through that person. Receive your parcel gracefully, without finding fault in that person. He or she is only a medium for delivering the parcel that was already due to you. If your mind grumbles, recognize the karmic lines you are forming and immediately seek forgiveness in your mind from God and from that person.

When you seek forgiveness or forgive someone, you are only doing a favor on yourself, not the other person. You are doing it to let yourself free from the bondage. If you love yourself and your freedom, you will perform the spiritual practice of forgiveness for liberation.

Seeker C: Yes Sirshree. I will perform this spiritual practice of forgiveness even if it's not my mistake. I will keep this understanding in my mind.

Sirshree: Also if you look at the incident from a higher level of consciousness, you will realize that the same Universal Self is acting through your body as well as the other person. So, whether you hurt someone or the other person hurts you, all transactions are happening for and between the Universal Self alone. It is the Self that is dealing with itself in and through all human beings. If you firmly believe in this inherent oneness and become aware of it in all your transactions, you will neither feel ashamed of seeking forgiveness nor allow ego or anger to prevent you from forgiving.

The real benefits of this practice cannot be conveyed just in words; it can only be felt through direct experience. When you keep yourself free from karmic lines and feel empty from within, you feel sublime and blissful. You don't experience any stress or burden on your mind. When you experience the power of emptiness, you begin to love it and you won't tolerate even a trace of karmic lines. It is then that the truest practice of forgiveness happens.

Seeker C: I understand it more clearly now. Since it is the Self or Consciousness that is involved in all dealings, it is the Self that is receiving all parcels. Forgiveness makes common sense.

Sirshree: With the right understanding of forgiveness, you will be able to respond in such a magnanimous manner that you may be surprised too. To understand this better, let us look at a story.

A hermit walked down a street every day at the same time. When he passed by a particular house, the woman of the house always got angry and dumped a bucketful of garbage on him from her balcony. But he peacefully continued on his way without reacting. This happened every day. Fed up with her mean nature, her son and daughter-in-law had left her long ago.

One day as the hermit went past her house, there was no flow of garbage from the balcony. The next day was the same. He wondered, "What's the matter with her? Why isn't she dumping garbage on me?" When he went to see her, he found that the woman was very sick and lying down helplessly.

He immediately called the doctor to treat her. He took great care of her. In a couple of days she completely recovered. The next day, as the hermit walked past her house as usual, the woman came down and fervently asked for forgiveness. He responded, "I forgave you on the very first day; it just touched you today!" She expressed her heartfelt gratitude and the next day, as he walked past, she came to him and offered him a cake. He lovingly accepted it and went his way.

Can you draw a parallel with your life using this example?

Seeker A: Despite repeated reminders, my housekeeper doesn't arrive on time. As soon as I see her, I just burst out at her. Now I realize that by entertaining negative thoughts and grumbling over her, I am forming karmic lines and getting myself bound by them. Instead, I should understand that nature is sending my parcel through her. I need to gracefully accept it. I should forgive her, thank her and move on to the next incident without clinging onto anything. Even if I grumble out of habit, I should immediately practice forgiveness to erase the karmic lines formed.

The hermit's consistent practice of forgiveness led him to behave kindly to the woman. I should allow my own practice to help me in the same way. As the woman changed her behavior, my maid also might change hers one day. But I will not practice forgiveness in anticipation of that.

Whether she arrives on time or not, I will continue with my practice. I will learn to maintain equanimity in both circumstances.

Sirshree: Good. This is important. Continue practicing forgiveness even if the situation doesn't change. Practice in order to erase the feelings that you are holding onto; not to force a favorable outcome. What examples do others have to share?

Seeker B: Whether it is somebody's bad driving that causes a traffic jam, or my boss reprimanding me for being late, I should consider the situation and the people involved just like the garbage dumping woman. I should gracefully accept the parcel with the conviction that if the parcel is delivered to me, it was meant to be mine. Nature has sent a parcel in the form of the situation and people are merely the medium to deliver it to me.

Seeker C: My neighbor always troubles me. He parks his car in front of my reserved parking space. Usually when I see it, I just fume and start abusing him. But now I will practice forgiveness. I will accept it as my parcel and forgive him. I will also seek forgiveness from him for my past behavior. This way I will erase the karmic lines and become free from the bondage of karma. I will be neutral whether he parks in front of my space or not. I will maintain equanimity in both circumstances.

Sirshree: Good contemplation! Whenever such garbage is dumped on you, always remember the hermit's response. If you practice forgiveness with complete understanding, the garbage will turn into cake. People will be amazed, "Wow, what has happened to him? He never gets angry now. He's always smiling and calm." Your calmness and poise will force them to think over their own behavior.

If you receive the garbage of hatred, anger, depression or guilt and you respond negatively or your mind starts grumbling, understand that a karmic line has started forming. Move the eraser of forgiveness over it, just like the hermit. No matter what the other person thinks of you, you have to continue the right behavior without hating, resenting or changing your emotions. No matter how you used to behave earlier, you have to take a new step now and enjoy the happiness that it brings. Though forgiveness may seem to be something you already know, the spiritual practice of forgiveness for liberation is very profound.

five

Seeker B: In a courtroom, the judge is presented with evidence and testimony and then delivers his verdict of justice. But the human mind is filled with cunningness, and lawyers manipulate the system, tamper with the evidence, and bribe the witnesses in order to influence the judgment. Many a time, the judge knows that the accused is the culprit, but he is forced to set him free due to inadequate evidence. The judge is helpless at the hands of the system. As a result, the culprit walks out free while the innocent goes to the jail. So how is this karmic judgment?

Sirshree: Karmic accounts are handled by the court of nature. And nature is not helpless like human judges. Nothing remains hidden from nature; it delivers impartial and accurate justice. It takes into account both visible and invisible facts.

For example, a poor person gets robbed of his hard-earned money. The loss is devastating and causes him mental trauma. Had a rich person been robbed for the same sum, the intensity of the trauma and the consequential effect would be different.

In the court of nature all such factors are considered before delivering justice. In addition to the actual money, the accompanying agony may be considered as part of the karmic account. Repayment may happen in the form of a penalty of money along with severe physical and mental trouble for the robber.

Seeker A: (laughs) This is quite interesting! No one can fool nature.

Sirshree: Indeed! When we are faced with difficulties, we feel that we are victimized by other people and try to blame fate or anyone else for our troubles. But the reality is that we have drawn karmic lines sometime or the other, the result of which has manifested in the form of troubles. Nature never does injustice to anyone as it is completely unbiased. To understand nature's fair dealing, let's understand the basics of karmic lines:

- Every action and reaction results in the formation of a karmic line and thereby a bondage.

- Not just outward action, but feelings, thoughts and speech result in the formation of karmic lines.

- Karmic lines are formed regardless of your positive or negative actions.

- The intention and feeling behind your action, and not the action itself, decides whether your karmic lines are good or bad, thick or thin.

Seeker B: Slowly I am able to grasp this subject. But still I am not able to understand nature's justice. In the earlier example, until the robber experiences physical and mental trouble along with loss of money, his karmic account can't be settled. So how does nature keep track of karmic accounts and the people involved in them?

Sirshree: That's beyond the grasp of the human intellect. Everything happens in an unseen realm. Whenever you create a line of bondage, you incur a liability. Nature preserves the liability in the form of a parcel tied with an invisible connection with this person. Until nature delivers this parcel, you feel burdened by the connection. It is nature's wisdom that decides when, how, and where parcels are delivered.

Seeker C: What kind of parcels are they?

Sirshree: Parcels can be delivered in any form. You may get them in the form of good feelings or bad. They may be in the form of a curse, an appreciation, or a complaint from someone. They may be in the form of feelings of accomplishment or failure, or in the form of objects you receive. They may be delivered while you are alone, surrounded by people, while you are at work, or when you are healthy or unhealthy. They may come in the form of lethargy or ignorance. When you feel good after helping someone, that good feeling is a parcel. When you feel regret, that too is a parcel. In short, whatever you receive in life is a parcel, created by you, sent by nature.

Seeker B: But how does nature deliver them all?

Sirshree: *Sometimes nature delivers the parcels directly and sometimes uses a medium.* The medium can be other people, incidents, or anything else for that matter.

Imagine, you are waiting for someone beside a road and a passer-by curses you. You also curse him back and grumble, wondering why he cursed you. Understand that the curse is a result of a past karmic line, which nature delivered using the medium of that person. The person is merely a courier. Now, your grumbling will create further karmic lines and later, you will get more parcels.

Seeker A: Do you mean to say that all the people and incidents in my life are due to my karmic lines only? They are the parcels created by me in the past and sent by nature?

Sirshree: Yes. Even though it may be hard to believe, this is the truth. *No power in the universe can give you someone else's parcel nor can your parcel be delivered to someone else.* It is only because of ignorance that people set the blame for their misfortunes on others.

Your thoughts, prayers, reactions, and feelings create good or bad karmic lines. When nature hands over the parcel through the medium of a human being or a situation, you shouldn't react to it, grumble over it, or sow a seed of bad feeling. Understand that your reactive karma draws another karmic line which incurs new liability. You will keep depositing your parcels with nature and nature will return them to you from time to time and the cycle will go on.

Seeker A: I always blame my spouse for my misfortune and grumble, "My spouse is unlucky for me. Ever since I got married, everything seems to be going wrong." But now I realize that nature has sent the parcel of past karmic lines using the medium of my spouse. The more I blame my spouse and grumble, the more I am getting bound by my karmic lines.

Sirshree: Good insight!

Seeker B: But I still wonder why I would create parcels that I'm not happy about?

Sirshree: This is the paradox. Nature doesn't create parcels based on your likes and dislikes. The moment you create karmic lines, your parcels are deposited with nature and nature delivers them in good time. But as time passes, you completely forget about them. Therefore, when nature returns the parcels in the form of appreciation, promotion or prosperity, you happily accept them. But when nature returns them in the form of criticism or demotion you feel bad and immediately complain, "Why do I always suffer? I can't understand why this is happening. I can't see where I could have gone wrong. It's my bad luck. The other person is the culprit for my misfortune."

Imagine the number of people you interact with every day. Usually, it's a fixed number of people. When you see someone, what kind of thoughts run through your mind? How do your feelings change from time to time? You may observe that your thoughts linger on some people. You constantly think good or bad about them. It's like you made them residential members in your mind. Can you think about the karmic lines you draw in the process?

Seeker B: When I drive to work, I get angry when someone passes me. If I'm stuck at a red light, I get frustrated. I internally fume at my boss when he gives me more work at the end of day. I lose my patience when I am stuck in traffic jams.

Seeker C: I argue when the shopkeepers don't return the correct change. I argue with the hawkers for selling vegetables and fruits at inflated prices. When I find that the lift is malfunctioning, I curse the administration.

Seeker A: I never thought about it this way. Every day I grumble about my housekeeper coming late. When unexpected guests arrive at home, I grumble. Despite multiple reminders, when my spouse forgets to buy things I asked for, I just burst out. When my children play when they should be studying, I scold them.

My God! Every day I meet so many people, commit so many transactions and really create lot of karmic lines. If all that happens over a course of one day, I can't imagine the number of karmic lines, and their effects, that I have created so far.

six

Seeker B: When I clearly see that someone is wrong, I sometimes feel the urge to point out where he is going wrong. Should I be mentally seeking forgiveness for such impulses? If I seek forgiveness for this impulsive urge, wouldn't it amount to feeling weak and cowardly?

Sirshree: Practicing forgiveness is not at all a sign of weakness, cowardice or helplessness. In fact, the tendency of nurturing anger and ego is a sign of weakness, cowardice and helplessness. It requires great strength to understand your anger and pacify it. You find it easier to think ill of others or to curse and to attack someone impulsively because you find it difficult to patiently look within your mind to observe your thinking pattern. It's a courageous act to understand others' feelings and be generous to them without serving your ego.

In fact, rendering forgiveness is a courageous act. Forgiving someone for his mistake and erasing the incident from the mind needs courage. It's easy to be rigid or quiet when we make mistakes. But keeping our ego aside, accepting our mistakes and seeking forgiveness from the bottom of our heart requires courage. Forgiveness is the cornerstone of courage. Despite having the power to punish, choosing to forgive and to pray for the liberation of others is not cowardice.

If you release this urge and still feel a need to give a feedback in service of a higher purpose, you can. But your action will be driven by the unbiased needs of the present rather than some emotion that is arising out of compulsion.

Whether or not the other person does, you will spiritually grow by seeking forgiveness for this urge. Forgiveness is the doorway to liberation. It helps you get free from your karmic lines and makes you pure, unblemished, calm and collected. It prepares you for the ultimate state of Self-realization.

Forgiveness is a divine quality. It is the portal into love – the basic nature of your true Self. When you forget your basic nature, you get entangled in defilements like anger, hatred, worry, stress and mental grumbling. However, when you start practicing forgiveness, these defilements vanish.

Seeker A: What if I commit a mistake and the other person doesn't forgive me and is always on the lookout for the opportunity to get even? Then, when he makes a mistake, I don't feel like forgiving him. If he hasn't forgiven me, why should I forgive him?

Sirshree: Some people consider forgiveness a transaction of give and take, but it isn't. If others don't forgive you, they draw karmic lines for themselves and they will receive their parcels from nature in due time. If you do the same, your parcels will arrive soon enough.

Remember, you are practicing forgiveness for your own liberation, not others'. If you don't want to compromise, then continue with your practice, no matter what others are doing.

Forgiveness is a source of joy. By forgiving, you get free from the associated karmic bondage. You easily accept the situation and remain detached from it, which allows you to become free from future distress or frustration arising from the situation. You live a life full of generosity, compassion, patience, contentment and happiness.

Seeker C: But there is a limit for tolerance. How long can I forgive the other person if he or she continues to misbehave with me?

Sirshree: It's natural to have such questions when you don't completely understand forgiveness. Always remember that you are receiving your parcels from nature through the medium of others. Those people have not created the parcel, you have. So instead of reacting to them, continue to practice forgiveness and gracefully accept all your parcels.

When you practice forgiveness, you become aware of your feelings in every situation. Instead of sowing seeds of negativity, try to sow seeds of faith and prayer. Awareness is the key to not develop any new karmic lines. If you create any unconsciously, instantly erase them through the practice of forgiveness. This way, you lead an awakened, aware and alert life.

Seeker C: Right. I used to believe that I tolerate the other person. But I now understand that my tolerance is actually toward my own parcels, which I need to accept gracefully.

Sirshree: You got it right. When you love yourself, you take responsibility for your spiritual practice of forgiveness. The idea is to keep your body healthy and mind pure by erasing karmic lines.

By practicing forgiveness, you nurture harmonious relationships with people. What fertilizers do for crops is what forgiveness does for relationships. Forgiveness helps relationships to grow and flourish. When you start loving others selflessly, you forgive them and seek forgiveness on their behalf in order to erase their karmic lines. You wish for them to experience the same joy that you are experiencing. The three mantras of Accept, Forgive and Let-go work magically in nurturing, strengthening and sweetening relationships.

Seeker B: Does that mean we should take responsibility for seeking forgiveness from everyone we interact with?

Sirshree: (laughs) Not only from the people you interact with, but also on behalf of all the people in the universe!

As you gain complete understanding of forgiveness, you take responsibility for the whole universe. The thoughts and karmic lines of all people collectively impact the universe. If a tragedy strikes somewhere, each of us is responsible for it to a small extent. Your practice can help reduce the burden on the Universal Self and the Earth. Today, a few people have assumed this responsibility and are selflessly practicing forgiveness and praying for world peace.

As you continue with the practice, you gain conviction that it is the Self (Consciousness) that manifests through everyone and as such, people are not the doers of their karma. A feeling of devotion grows, which makes you happily practice forgiveness for everyone. In the process, you become free from your karmic lines and grow spiritually.

In one of his couplets, the saint Kabir has said, "Where there is kindness, there is order; where there is greed, there is sin. Where there is anger, there is hell and where there is forgiveness, there is God." Look at it this way – God is enacting forgiveness through you.

Seeker B: I understand the collective impact of everyone's thoughts and karmic lines on the Self and the Earth. Whenever I have lunch with co-workers, we tend to complain, blaming the government for bad roads, garbage on the streets, traffic jams, corruption, and so on. Sometimes they blame their family for extravagant expenses, lack of comfort, convenience or peace. I always join them in these discussions. But now I realize that this forms karmic lines and impacts the entire universe. I won't participate in such discussions anymore. Instead, I will practice forgiveness on their behalf.

Sirshree: Good! If you are a true seeker wanting to know the nature of the Self, you will practice forgiveness and not indulge in behaviors like that. If you are in favor of love, you will practice forgiveness.

We all know the laws and regulations of the world because we grew up with them, hear them all around us. It's a different matter how many of us actually follow them. But the laws of our inner world (the world of thoughts) are neither visible nor audible. If only few people follow the laws of the visible world, how many would follow the laws of the unseen world?

It's difficult to understand and believe in what is invisible because no one teaches us or reminds us about them. Only those who have complete faith in their guru or the Higher Self or the Universe or God will truly understand. For them, everything in life becomes easy and smooth. They work on awareness of their thoughts and mental habits, perform prayers and most importantly, perform the spiritual practice of forgiveness. As a result, they see changes automatically happening in the outer world as a reflection of changes happening within them. They don't need to act tough or have any friction with people.

If you wish to live a stress-free life with ease, follow the laws of thought and practice forgiveness. If you are awakened, you will automatically practice forgiveness. If two people have a fight, who is most likely to seek forgiveness? It is the awakened one who is aware and understands his responsibility for himself and for others.

Those who are not awakened, blame others and count their mistakes. If you always hold someone else responsible for all your problems, then what is your role? Is it to blame others for their faults? No! Your responsibility is to examine yourself and observe whether you are knowingly or unknowingly contributing towards these mistakes.

seven

Seeker A: Sirshree, what is the right way to seek or give forgiveness? Do we have to actually say sorry or can we say it mentally?

Sirshree: Forgiveness is an inner quality. It is a feeling that arises from the bottom of the heart. Just saying the words "I'm sorry" to someone as a passing remark, or saying it in your mind as a ritual isn't the right way of seeking forgiveness. Also, if you simply say, "I forgive you" to someone but hold onto your feelings of hatred or anger, then this is not the right way to forgive. What you feel in your heart is more important than whether you say it out loud or not.

If you are comfortable asking for forgiveness through direct interaction, you may say, "Please forgive me for the hurt I caused you through my feelings, thoughts, words or actions." You may also add, "I will ensure that I won't repeat the mistake again."

At the very least, attempt to seek forgiveness directly from your loved ones. By coming face to face with the concerned person and seeking forgiveness, the mind gets cleansed immediately. The clouds of sadness, anger and doubt hovering over your relationship will vanish. When one person seeks forgiveness, the other person may realize his or her fault.

Seeker C: But what if it's the other person's fault and he is too adamant to accept it?

Sirshree: The ego often blocks the path of forgiveness. But once you take the first step, the ego drops and the blockage clears. Then both of you reconcile and the karmic lines are instantly erased.

But if the other cannot take the first step, you should take the lead and seek forgiveness in order to maintain the sweetness in your relationship and not to let the matter escalate. This will help the other person loosen up and realize his or her role in the standoff. The chances are good that the other person could say, "It was my fault as well. Please forgive me." The molehill doesn't turn into a mountain and the road to reconciliation opens up.

Even if the other person is not ready to forgive you, don't assume that this standoff will remain forever. Understand that his 'no' actually means "not now." He or she is telling you, "Right now I cannot forgive you." After some time, ask for forgiveness again. Maybe this time the response will be different. Remember you are not seeking forgiveness for his or her approval; you are doing it to cleanse yourself and to help him release the feeling of hatred.

Again, you can also choose to seek forgiveness mentally. Once you do this, things loosen up in your mind and you shift to happiness. Happiness begets more happiness.

Seeker B: How do we seek forgiveness mentally and when?

Sirshree: In many situations, you don't feel comfortable asking for forgiveness directly. And in many other situations, you realize very late that you made a mistake. In such situations, you can practice forgiveness through a mental prayer. Close your eyes and follow these steps:

Invite: *Dear divine form of………. (say the person's name), I am inviting you into my field of awareness.*

Forgive: *I am letting go of the hatred, resentment or complaint that I have in my mind against you. With God (or guru or any source of inspiration) as my witness, I forgive you. I love you and respect you.*

Seek forgiveness: *With God (or guru or any source of inspiration) as my witness, I seek your forgiveness. I seek your forgiveness for considering you a body, separate from me. I failed to acknowledge the presence of Higher Consciousness, the Self, within you. I will not commit this mistake again. Please forgive me for holding negative thoughts or feelings or for the hurt I caused you through my words or actions.*

Express gratitude: *Thank you very much for being in my field of awareness. Thank you. Thank you. Thank you.*

Seeker C: I interact with so many people during the course of a day. I tend to unintentionally hurt them when I am not aware of my feelings, thoughts, words or actions. Do I need to perform this prayer every time this happens?

Sirshree: Whenever you have a feeling of hatred or a complaint against someone in your mind, or whenever you feel you have erred in action, perform this prayer immediately to erase the bondage of karma. Make it a rule to at least do it at bedtime by recalling all the incidents from the day. Become big-hearted and seek forgiveness from those with whom you formed a karmic bondage by harboring a feeling of hatred, resentment or anger. Pray for their wellbeing. Don't leave any karmic bondage for the next day.

When you erase each and every karmic line the same day it is created, past thoughts will not trouble you the next day. Just like a homemaker cleans the kitchen before going to bed so that the next day she feels cheerful when she enters the kitchen and she can start each day fresh. Similarly, you also need to clean your mind before going to bed.

Every night before going to bed, forgive all and seek forgiveness from those whom you might have hurt knowingly or unknowingly. When you wake up in the morning with a big and open heart, spread love to everyone. Treat each day as if you had a huge treasure chest of gold coins that you are gifting to everyone you meet. Fill your heart with love and gift this love to everyone. Make this a daily practice and you will soon see the results.

You will find your relationships are directly affected. In a few days you will say to yourself, "Wow! The people who used to ignore me now treat me kindly. My relationships are now improving. Problems are automatically getting solved. Everything in life is coming to me so easily and spontaneously. And on top of all this, I feel peaceful within."

This happens because your karmic bondages are dissolving and you are becoming free. All this starts in the invisible realm. People don't believe it easily and hence they don't begin the practice. But those who practice, witness miracles in their lives.

Outwardly, you may feel that you are forgiving and seeking forgiveness from many people, but the truth is that you seek forgiveness from only one entity and forgive only this one entity. If you understand this clearly, you will feel no hesitation in forgiving or seeking forgiveness from anyone.

Seeker B: What is this entity?

Sirshree: Call it God, the Higher Self, universal energy, Allah, Krishna, or Supreme Consciousness. It is the enlivening principle in whose presence the entire universe is functioning and being sustained. Behind, within and around every animate and inanimate thing – whether visible or invisible, whether gross or subtle – is God, or Consciousness.

Consciousness, or God, is the background of everything and is part of everything too. When you seek forgiveness from anyone, including yourself, understand that you are actually seeking forgiveness from Consciousness. In fact, it is Consciousness that is asking for forgiveness through you to become free from karmic bondage and blossom completely – through you!

From now on, whenever you seek forgiveness from anyone, be aware that you're seeking forgiveness not from the individual, but from God. People seek forgiveness before idols and various deities. This helps them to concentrate and to evoke feelings of devotion. Lord Ganesha, Lord Krishna, Lord Shiva, Allah, or Jesus are all representatives of the one God who cleanses our karmic lines. We can refer to it as God of Dusting, GoD.

Seeker C: I really appreciate the way our ancestors have ingrained the quality of forgiveness in many of our customs and traditions. Elders used to write, "Forgive me for my shortcomings," at the end of letters. When they woke up in the morning, they used to worship the ground before stepping on it. Before plucking fruits or flowers, they used to worship the plant. If they accidentally stepped on a book or any inanimate object, they used to seek forgiveness from it by reverently touching it. At the end of every Hindu ritual, a mantra for forgiveness is always chanted. In Jainism, a festival is dedicated to practice forgiveness, which goes on for several days.

Sirshree: The true meaning of some of these customs was lost as they were passed down to the next generation, which is why they gradually died out. Today the practice of seeking forgiveness from non-living objects or from nature has largely disappeared.

But now you understand the importance of practicing forgiveness. Consciousness is all-pervading. It is present in all humans, animals, birds, plants, and inanimate objects. When you know this clearly, you won't shy away from seeking forgiveness from all these forms, including your body.

Nature sends our karmic parcels in different forms through various mediums. When we practice forgiveness after receiving them, we are cleansed of our karmic bondages. When we are completely cleansed, we become an empty flute that plays divine music. We revel in the bliss of love, joy and peace. Then the Self can express through our body-mind without any blocks. The most wondrous creations happen through beings where the ego has surrendered to God and has opened up to the expression of divinity.

In order to achieve this state, you need to be aware and alert in the present without repeating the mistakes of the past. Whenever you remember past karmic lines, seek forgiveness from God. If you consistently practice this, your level of consciousness will rise and you will be able to discern the truth. You will be more sensitive and receptive to divine intuition.

You can understand how to become free from the burden of the past and remain in the present through a story:

Lord Buddha was preaching in a village, "Become forgiving and tolerant like Mother Earth. Holding onto anger is like grasping red-hot coal with the intent of throwing it at someone else. You are the one who gets burned. Anger is a mental disorder, a sign of weakness. It can never be justified or called natural."

Among the listeners was a man with a short fuse. He used to get angry at the slightest provocation and used to always blame others for the situation. That day, he had a fight with his wife and he was in a very foul mood. He had come for the teaching to seek solace.

But as soon as he heard Buddha's words, he flared up. He found the teaching wrong and hollow. He stood up and started yelling. But the Buddha only listened to him. His eyes were full of compassion and peace. The man thought that Lord Buddha would reciprocate in the same manner but he didn't react or say anything. So he became more furious. He hurled more and more abuses at the Buddha and stormed out.

The next day, when he calmed down, he felt remorse for what he had done. He was ashamed of his behavior and overcome with guilt and anxiety for having insulted a Self-realized saint like the Buddha. He feared for the repercussions of his dreadful sin.

He immediately went to the place where Lord Buddha was staying. But the Buddha had moved on to another village. The man was desperate to seek forgiveness and so began walking without bothering to have his meal. For hours he walked from one village to another. His body was exhausted, but he didn't give up. Finally, he found the Buddha sitting under a tree. He fell at his feet, "Please forgive me."

The Buddha replied, "Who are you, brother? Why are you asking for forgiveness?"

The man said, "Lord, I am the same person who insulted you yesterday in a fit of rage. I have realized my mistake. I am literally burning in the fire of remorse. Please forgive this disgraceful person that I am."

The Buddha lovingly replied, "Friend, I don't remember what happened yesterday. Today you are seeking forgiveness, but even this is temporary. I have already left the past behind and you should too. You have realized your mistake and you have expressed remorse. You have also learned a lesson on how anger destroys your sanity and makes you do wrong things. Remember this lesson and let go of the past. Remain in the present from now on. This is the right way to live."

Just like the man in the story, learn the lessons from the past and let go of your regrets. Always carry the torch of forgiveness and move ahead in life, enjoying the present. As soon as something troubles your mind, practice forgiveness.

eight

Seeker A: I sought forgiveness from my spouse. He also reciprocated by seeking forgiveness. We have put the matter behind us and are in harmony. But now I feel overwhelmed with regret for how I behaved. I feel I should have been mature. How can I deal with this?

Sirshree: It's very easy to blame others. But when we point one finger at another, we forget that three fingers point back at us. While pinpointing faults in others, we rarely pay attention to our own faults, tendencies and shortcomings. We are so preoccupied with blaming and shaming, that we don't take an honest look at ourselves. The truth is that unless we forgive ourselves, we cannot forgive others.

For every wrong action that has happened through you so far, seek forgiveness from GoD and pray:

Dear GoD,

Please help me to forgive myself.

Please help me to cleanse myself within.

Please help me to accept myself.

Please help me to love myself.

Please purify my inner being.

Tell yourself, "I forgive you. I forgive you for all that has happened so far. I forgive you for all the karmic lines formed, knowingly and unknowingly. Let God forgive me. Thank you. Thank you. Thank you."

Feel the state of being forgiven and experience a radical transformation within. It's as if a great burden has been lifted and you experience lightness.

Sometimes, you may be overwhelmed with so much guilt that it seems impossible to forgive yourself. If you haven't gained complete clarity about forgiveness, your mind may entangle you at certain places. These entanglements allow you to feel justified about not practicing forgiveness. When this happens, instead of wasting your time and effort in arguing with your mind, set that particular situation aside. Practice forgiveness in all the other areas where you have gained clarity. Once you are done with this, go back and work on other situations.

Seeker A: I always feel that my brother neglects me and isn't cordial with me. Somehow, I feel that he has antipathy towards me. I don't feel like I can connect with him.

Sirshree: If someone doesn't like you, thinks bad about you, and does bad things to you, you probably have bad feelings for him in return. It almost feels natural. But in reality, the feeling of hatred is not a natural response. It's a mechanically programmed response.

As you learn the method of gaining complete freedom from karmic lines, you should stop reacting mechanically. Don't harbor the same old feelings as you used to. In fact, you should not only forgive him to cleanse him of his hurtful tendencies, but also seek forgiveness on his behalf from GoD and pray:

Dear GoD,

Please forgive both of us.

Please purify us from within.

Please cleanse our minds.

Seeker A: I am ready to seek forgiveness if it's my fault. But why should I seek forgiveness if it's my brother's fault?

Sirshree: You should seek forgiveness because you assumed him to be an individual with a limited body-mind mechanism. You did not see the all-pervading Universal Self within him. You should seek forgiveness from GoD for this mistake of yours and pray:

Dear GoD,

Please forgive me.

Despite having received this wisdom,

I still consider people as separate individuals.

I failed to see your divine presence within them.

Instead I saw an individual, with ego and hatred.

It was my incorrect perception.

Please forgive me for my fault.

Please forgive both of us.

As soon as you pray for forgiveness, you feel as if those particular karmic lines are cleansed from within. This also triggers the cleansing, or at least lightening, of the associated karmic lines within your brother. It's as if those snakes are erased from the game board. You will be surprised to see a pleasant change in his approach and behavior towards you.

When you seek forgiveness on behalf of others for their karma, your relationship with them becomes better and more pure than before. You need to witness this miracle for yourself. The more you experience it, the greater your conviction in the efficacy of acceptance and forgiveness will be.

Seeker B: One of my friends shared with me that her husband has started indulging in alcohol because of the differences and constant arguments between them. I was sharing with her that she could practice forgiveness to resolve this situation.

Sirshree: Very true! There is no better ointment than acceptance and forgiveness for such deep wounds. Without it, people fall prey to addictions like alcohol, smoking, and many more, in the vain attempt of getting rid of their sorrow. People don't realize that addictions won't bring long-term pleasure. They invite suffering in the guise of pleasure.

But those who have gained this wisdom will never commit such a misstep. We need to learn to practice forgiveness the way Lord Mahavir and Lord Buddha did. Let others draw as many karmic lines as they want, but do not let their impressions fall upon you. Whatever be the karma of others, you don't have to react to them. Always respond in a new, fresh and aware manner by being in the present moment.

Seeker B: When this friend of mine shares her inner feelings and sorrows with me, I try to pacify her and help her in whatever way I can. She feels better and lighter but I end up feeling disheartened and drained in the process. I don't know why this happens to me.

Sirshree: When you listen to her, you get attached to her sorrows. You become sad and depressed. As a result, your level of consciousness drops. Generally, when you grieve over the sorrow of another, it seems as if you are showing sympathy and love towards her. But that's not real love. By doing that, you are unknowingly acknowledging her sorrow as the truth and allowing it to intensify.

Some mothers are so emotionally attached to their children that when the children fall sick, they also fall sick by being sad and worried for them. This makes things worse at home. How can they help their children recover if they themselves are not in a right frame of mind?

When you feel sympathetic looking at a sad and depressed person, you say, "Why did such a thing happen to her? She is so sad! Why does God do this to good people?" You repeatedly use words like unfortunate, sad, or worried to describe her sorrowful and pitiful state in detail. You want to help, but you fail to realize that by describing her sorrowful state, you have unknowingly invited more sorrow for her and made the situation worse.

A law of nature states: *Whatever you describe turns into reality.* The law of nature never fails; it does its job relentlessly.

Be aware and alert in such situations. Seek forgiveness from GoD on her behalf and pray:

Dear GoD,

Please forgive her for becoming sad.

Please cleanse the karmic lines that are entangling her.

If you grieve over the sorrow of the other person, seek forgiveness from GoD for you too. By doing this, you will cancel your negative contribution.

Dear GoD,
Please forgive me.
Despite having received this wisdom
I considered my friend a separate individual and
increased her sorrow by thinking negatively for her.
I failed to see your divine presence within her.
Please forgive me for my incorrect perception.
Please forgive both of us.

Seeker C: I always think logically and try to understand what is right and what is wrong. As a result, I am always in a confused state.

Sirshree: Until your mind is completely surrendered to God, you cannot understand certain things entirely. The mind always wishes to be logical and classifies everything as right or wrong. But certain things become clear to you only when you have begun to cleanse your karmic lines through the practice of forgiveness. Whenever your mind is confused and you are at a loss to understand certain things, pray to GoD for clarity:

Dear GoD,
Please erase my karmic lines that arise out of ignorance
and create blocks and doubts in my understanding.
I don't know what it is that I need to understand, but you do.
Please eliminate those things that I need not know and
that are obstacles in my journey towards the Truth.
Please help me receive and understand whatever I need to know.
I am open to receive.

Let Thy will be mine.
Thank you. Thank you. Thank you.

Seeker C: Lately, I have been sick quite often. I want to be healthy. After listening to you, I have been analyzing which karmic lines could have caused this, whether they are recent or formed in the distant past. But I'm still not clear.

Sirshree: Don't worry about when the karmic lines were formed, about what their nature is, or how they will affect you. Just focus on erasing them by practicing forgiveness. Whenever you experience a negative feeling, instead of trying to figure out why you're feeling it, understand that it is due to a karmic line and immediately erase it through the practice of forgiveness.

Through prayer, ask God to give you an indication of the topics you need clarity in. If you want to be healthy, but don't know how to go about it, you can pray to GoD:

Dear GoD,
You know what is good for me and what is not.
Please remove all unnecessary elements
like unhealthy food from my life.
Please grant me good health and vitality.
I am ready to receive and
abide by whatever you choose for me.
Let Thy will be mine.
Thank you. Thank you. Thank you.

Surrender the reins of your life to God and be receptive to the things that He sends. Keep your doorway open to God. Help divine things reach you, by letting go of your mind's negative self-talk. If you do this, there is nothing that can stop God's grace from reaching you. You will receive health, knowledge, success, bliss, peace, love and joy.

nine

Seeker C: I've been performing the spiritual practice of forgiveness – just like you have taught. But somehow I feel it's not effective.

Sirshree: What exactly do you do as part of the practice?

Seeker C: Whenever I feel negative, I repeat the prayers you shared in order to erase karmic lines. Before going to bed, I seek and give forgiveness from everyone I interacted with throughout the day.

Sirshree: How do you feel during the practice?

Seeker C: I just repeat the prayers without paying much attention to my feelings. And I experience a lot of resistance within when seeking forgiveness from some people.

Sirshree: It's good that you are sincerely practicing forgiveness. But to make it more effective you need to develop certain qualities within. Treat them as the pillars of the practice of forgiveness.

Seeker B: What are they?

Sirshree: Feeling is the first quality. Feeling is the language of God. When you pray, God considers your feelings, not words. When you practice forgiveness, speak your prayers with deep genuine feeling. If you just repeat the words, "I forgive you" without infusing them with genuine feelings and continue to hold onto your hurt, you may find that the prayer is not effective. *Praying without feelings reduces its effectiveness.*

Seeker B: Sometimes, I experience resistance within when I pray. I am not comfortable with certain words in the prayer.

Sirshree: When you experience resistance while praying, the prayer isn't coming from the bottom of your heart; you just say it out of force. But when the prayer is free flowing, it touches your heart. Always use words you are comfortable with, because that will help you express your feelings. Before beginning, say the prayer:

Dear GoD,

Let my prayer be full of genuine feelings.

Let it produce the highest results.

This story teaches us the importance of feeling during prayer:

There was a priest who lived in a beautiful church on the banks of a river. One day he heard that three hermits, who lived on the other side of the river, taught people how to pray. People from the nearby villages flocked to learn from them. The priest became sad as the hermits became more popular. He wondered, "Even though I am right here, people make so much effort to cross river to meet the hermits? What prayer are they learning?"

One day, he ferried across the river to meet the hermits. He asked them, "What prayer do you teach people?" The hermits replied, "You are three, we are three, please forgive us." The priest burst into laughter, "Is this a prayer? How strange! This is not what a prayer should be like." The hermits replied, "Perhaps we don't know what a prayer should be like. Will you teach us the right prayer?"

The priest agreed. He asked them to memorize a long prayer with many flowery words and stanzas. The hermits tried, but they would forget and then recollect it with great difficulty only to forget it again. Finally, after a great deal of effort, the father helped them to memorize the prayer. He then crossed the river back to his church.

When he reached the middle of the river, he heard someone calling out to him from the river bank. He saw the three hermits waving to him and running on water – without a boat! When they reached the father, they pleaded with him, "Father, please forgive us. We forgot the prayer again. Please teach us once again." But the priest was stunned to realize the power that they had acquired through their spiritual practice.

He told them, "You don't need to learn my long prayer. Your short prayer is good enough. It has immense power. You are three, we are three, please forgive us."

The prayer can be made even shorter by removing "You are three, we are three," from it. The short prayer "Please forgive us," is enough if you have pure and genuine feelings behind it. Asking for forgiveness is a profound true prayer because it liberates us from karmic bondages and leads us to love, joy and peace.

The words that the hermits used in their prayer were irrelevant. What mattered was their feeling, which was all-inclusive. This gave their prayer immense power and fulfillment.

Seeker C: Thank you. I realize my mistake. I need to practice forgiveness with genuine feelings. Just repeating the words is pointless.

Sirshree: Don't let this become an excuse for the mind to stop the practice. Don't allow this to become a hurdle. If the feeling is missing, continue the practice of repeating words. Make sure that you understand this practice fully. Be clear about the meaning of the forgiveness prayer and the feeling will follow in due course of time.

Seeker C: I chant prayers in Sanskrit everyday but I don't know their meaning. I'll continue with my chanting but try to understand their meaning.

Sirshree: Yes, this is important. Then the feeling will arise within you. When people chant prayers, mantras, or verses without understanding their meaning, it's of no use. Then they complain to God that He doesn't hear them. The truth is that God receives your feelings, not words. If you have not expressed your feelings, how can He fulfill them?

Seeker B: Sorry Sirshree, but I still have some doubts about the way forgiveness works. If I seek forgiveness within my mind, how will the other person know about it? How will he forgive me and how will I receive his forgiveness in return? How will I get free from my karmic bondages? How does it really work?

Sirshree: The spiritual practice of forgiveness works in the invisible realm. Those who think logically find it hard to believe the invisible reality.

Faith is the second quality. When you seek forgiveness from GoD, have complete faith that your prayers are being listened to and will be answered, the laws of nature are always working. Your faith will empower your prayer. Here is another story to help you understand this:

In a remote village there lived a tribal man who suffered from severe stomach pain. He learned that there was a very good doctor in the city who could cure his ailment. He travelled to the city and reached the doctor's home early in the morning. The doctor woke up from his sleep and attended to the man. He concluded that the only way to cure him was stomach surgery. He wanted to be sure, so he asked the man to visit his clinic later in the day for scans and tests.

The villager replied, "No, I don't know the roads here. I don't know where your clinic is and I don't have enough money for the treatment. I can't visit your clinic. Please give me some medicine now and I will go away."

The doctor was in a fix. "What should I do now? This man doesn't understand the severity of his illness and he doesn't have money for treatment." Since the villager was so adamant, he wrote a prescription and handed it over. "Take this medicine for 21 days." The villager happily took the paper, thanked the doctor profusely and went home.

After 21 days, the villager returned to the doctor and said, "Thank you so much! Your medicine has completely cured my stomach pain. I am well again!" The doctor was surprised that he had recovered without surgery. He couldn't even remember which medicine he had prescribed.

"Can you show me the prescription I gave you?" The villager asked, "Which paper?" The doctor replied, "The one with the name of the medicine." The villager was dumbfounded, "Oh! That paper?! But didn't you tell me to take it for 21 days? I tore the paper into 21 bits and had a bite each day. It has completely cured me."

The villager ate the prescription paper believing it to be the medicine. Because he had complete faith in the doctor and his medicine, he was cured. This is the power of faith. His faith made the impossible possible. People often fail to recover from illnesses in spite of taking the right medicine. This is because they lack faith in the medicine. They doubt its efficacy or the competency of the doctor. The villager had no doubt. He knew that if the doctor said so, it would happen, even if the medicine were just a piece of paper.

Those who know the power of faith have no hesitation in infusing their prayers with deep feelings just like the mistaken villager. Such people get amazing results in life.

In order to erase karmic lines of doubt and increase faith, pray:

Dear GoD,
I favor faith, not doubt.
Please forgive me for doubting.
Please remove all the obstacles that weaken my faith.
Let my faith become unswerving and unconditional.
Thank you. Thank you. Thank you.

ten

Seeker A: Somehow, it seems I'm practicing forgiveness for the same mistakes. Although I decide to not repeat these mistakes, I commit them unconsciously.

Sirshree: The third essential quality of the practice of forgiveness is alertness. If you are not alert while seeking forgiveness, you will not harness its full benefit. If you are seeking forgiveness, it means you have recognized your fault. Once you recognize your fault, you also need to be aware of removing it. Otherwise, in spite of seeking forgiveness, you will continue to repeat the same mistake, by force of habit.

Suppose you are suffering from a backache. Every night before going to bed, you seek forgiveness from your back for not taking care of it and promise to look after it properly from now on. But the very next day, you fall right back into your mechanical way of living. Unconsciously, you bend your back in the wrong way, put unnecessary stress on it, and so on. Again at night you seek forgiveness from it in the hope that it will recover on its own.

Your back can take care of itself and recover on its own, if you don't burden it with more stress and give it a chance to recover. Awareness plays an important role here. Along with the practice of forgiveness, be aware of your actions, words, thoughts and feelings. Live an alert and aware life. Don't repeat the same mistakes again and again.

In order to raise your level of awareness and erase the karmic lines formed out of unconsciousness, pray:

Dear GoD,

I favor awakened awareness, not unconsciousness.

I favor wisdom, not ignorance.

Please forgive me for my unconscious awareness.

Please forgive me for the tendencies that make me unconscious.

Please remove these tendencies from my body-mind.

Please cleanse me from within, please forgive me.

Thank you. Thank you. Thank you.

Seeker B: I have been practicing forgiveness but somehow I am not consistent with the practice.

Sirshree: In fact, **consistency is the fourth, and the most essential, quality of forgiveness.** Without it, not even your excellence with the other qualities will bring you any benefit. If you have consistency, you can gradually develop the other qualities. Do you know Aesop's fable about the race between the tortoise and the hare? In spite of being much slower than the hare, the tortoise wins the race and makes the impossible possible because of its consistency.

In ignorance, you have been creating karmic lines since childhood. Now that you understand the importance and the need of practicing forgiveness, you have to be consistent to erase these lines. Also, raise your awareness to prevent new lines. Just like persistent axe blows can bring down the biggest tree, consistently practicing forgiveness can erase the deepest of karmic bondages. It can break apart the thick bundle of karmic lines.

Whenever you realize the need or whenever you get an opportunity, immediately practice forgiveness. Make it a habit to practice it every night at bedtime. Even realizing the lack of consistency in your practice is a good beginning. In order to erase the karmic lines of laziness and develop consistency in your practice, pray:

Dear GoD,

I favor consistency, not hurdles.

Please eliminate the obstacles to my consistent practice of forgiveness.

I don't know what the obstacles are.

They could be a tendency, a false belief or some old thought.

*Whatever it is, please forgive me for the
karmic line created because of it.*

Please erase and cleanse my karmic lines from within.

Thank you. Thank you. Thank you.

If you start performing this prayer daily, you will develop consistency quickly.

Seeker C: I practice forgiveness from the bottom of my heart with a genuine feeling but I wonder when I will see any benefit from it.

Sirshree: Total surrender is the fifth quality of forgiveness. Practice forgiveness with the same feeling of surrender that a farmer has for his soil. The farmer sows seeds in the soil and helps to create the best conditions to support their germination. With a feeling of complete surrender, he leaves it to nature to do its job at the appropriate time.

Similarly, when you practice forgiveness with anyone, it's like practicing it with God. Each time, you are sowing seeds of prayer with God. Surrender your prayers to the hands of God. You may not be aware, but He knows what is good for you and what is essential for you. Leave it to Him to determine when, how and in what way He should fulfill your prayers. Rest assured that He will complete them at the appropriate time. Experience now the same joy and satisfaction that you will feel after your prayers are fulfilled.

At the end of each prayer, with a feeling of complete surrender, say to GoD:

Let Thy will be mine.

This is the mantra to develop total surrender to God.

SECTION II

Causes of Karmic Bondage

eleven

Seeker C: Yesterday, I went to see an art exhibition. Looking at the pieces on display was exciting, and one of the paintings caught my attention. When I looked closer, I was disappointed with the color. Without thinking I remarked spontaneously, "What a horrible color! The whole painting has been spoiled. Who is the stupid painter?" But then I considered that I might have perhaps created a karmic line. Do such trivial comments create karmic lines?

Sirshree: Yes, it does. Unconscious remarks create karmic lines that bind you. We are not charged for the words we speak, and so we use, or rather misuse, our speech in any way we like. But our words act like a boomerang. If our words are full of love, they bring back love and if they are hateful, they bring back hate to us.

A famous example of karmic lines that develop from words is that of Draupadi in the Indian epic Mahabharata. Draupadi was married to five brothers, the Pandavas, who built a grand palace full of amusing illusions. They invited their cousins, the Kauravas, to visit. Duryodhana, the eldest of the Kauravas, was amazed at the illusions. He tried to enter what looked like a pool of water, but was surprised to find that it was the optical illusion of a glass floor. Then, he tried to walk across what looked like a tiled floor but was actually a pool of water. He fell and was drenched in water. Draupadi burst into laughter at this sight and remarked, "The blind son of a blind father…"

Duryodhana was so enraged that ultimately it culminated into a war, the Mahabharata! Draupadi's words created karmic lines. As a result, she had to suffer humiliation at the court of Duryodhana. The war of Mahabharata was set into motion; the negative events of the war continued to create more karmic lines.

You never know how your words impact others. Unconsciously, you may make some passing remarks to a stranger in a traffic jam, to an assistant at work, to one of your children playing truant at school, or even about someone whom you don't know directly, like the painter in your case. But your casual words may offend the other person. They will create karmic lines and you will receive the corresponding parcel from nature in time. It is important to choose your words wisely.

Seeker C: I speak whatever I feel. I may have hurt many people with my words. How can I change this habit?

Sirshree: Before you open your mouth to say something, think about what you want to say. Evaluate whether they will create any form of karmic line and, if so, avoid speaking them. Take the following precautions:

- Never say something that might hurt another.
- Never say anything provocative.
- Never criticize a third person in his or her absence.
- Never use negative words.
- Never say anything that might depress another.
- Never taunt or express anger at anyone.

Seeker B: Thank you for showing us how to avoid creating new karmic lines. But what should we do about things we have already said and the karmic lines created from that?

Sirshree: Just as you use an eraser to erase a chalkboard, similarly use the eraser of forgiveness to erase your old lines. Sit calmly and recall the words you've used in the past which might have created karmic lines. It would be best if you seek forgiveness directly. This will instantly mend your relationship. If it's not possible, seek forgiveness at the mental level. Close your eyes and follow these steps:

Invite: *Dear divine form of.......... (say the person's name), I am inviting you into my field of awareness.*

Seek forgiveness: *With God (or guru or any source of inspiration) as my witness, I seek your forgiveness. Please forgive me for the hurt I knowingly or unknowingly caused you through my words. I also seek your forgiveness for considering you a body separate from me. I failed to acknowledge the presence of Consciousness, the Self, within you. I will ensure not to say anything that might hurt you. I will not repeat this mistake again.*

Express gratitude: *Thank you very much for being in my field of awareness and for forgiving me. I love you. I respect you. Thank you. Thank you. Thank you.*

Seeker A: But sometimes my son doesn't listen to me. He wants to play when he should be doing his homework. When he won't listen, I scold him.

Sirshree: Sometimes a teacher must speak to the students harshly and a mother needs to be stern with her child. In situations like this, be aware and avoid being angry or hateful when you are talking. Say whatever you have to say and immediately practice forgiveness at a mental level with that person in order to erase the karmic lines formed.

twelve

Seeker B: Yesterday, I promised to take my wife for shopping in the evening. That afternoon my boss asked me if I could complete an urgent task that needed to be finished the same day. I assured him that I would take care of it. He was happy and grateful for my flexibility. Although outwardly I agreed, my mind was preoccupied with resentful thoughts, "He is always the thorn in my happiness. Now, I will have to deal with my wife's anger and complaints!" It took a long time for me to complete the work and when I reached home it was late. And I couldn't take my wife shopping. She was upset with me. Though I didn't say anything to my boss, did my thoughts create karmic lines?

Sirshree: Even though you didn't say anything directly to your boss, you said it to yourself and so you are bound by karmic lines with your boss.

This is an example of self-talk. Self-talk happens in your mind and then sometimes you speak those thoughts out loud. Muttering to yourself, grumbling to yourself, pondering why something did not go the way you wanted to – is all self-talk. Since your self-talk is incessant throughout the day, it produces a vast number of karmic lines. Be aware of your self-talk and ensure that it's always positive.

Seeker C: But, I am not cursing anyone directly. I am only thinking to myself. What is wrong with that? I haven't hurt anyone.

Sirshree: You are saying this because you haven't understood the effect of self-talk. When you think negatively about someone, you draw a karmic line for yourself. If you repeatedly think negatively, it may become your reality. You will accumulate karmic lines and someday these lines will force you to do wrong things. Karmic lines arising out of negative self-talk make the mind unhealthy and this could even lead to diseases in the body. Your mental and physical health are affected by negative self-talk; so you harm yourself instead of the other person in the process.

Seeker A: How can we ensure that our self-talk always remains positive?

Sirshree: Although self-talk is internal to your mind, it acts as a gateway to control your behavior and actions in the world outside. Be vigilant about what seeds of feelings you are sowing in your mind. What you sow, so you reap. If you sow the feelings of sadness, negativity, depression, irritation or anger, they will create negative karmic lines. As soon as you sense these feelings, understand that your self-talk has become negative.

Whatever be the problem, make it a rule that you will respond lovingly, peacefully and politely. To do that you need to have the same feelings in your self-talk. To the extent that you practice forgiveness, your mind becomes permeated with love, joy and peace. This, in turn, positively affects your self-talk.

Seeker B: How can I erase the karmic lines formed due to my negative self-talk?

Sirshree: As soon as you realize that negative self-talk is happening in your mind, pray:

Dear GoD,

Please forgive me for my negative self-talk.

Please help me avoid negative self-talk from now on.

Give me strength to have positive self-talk, full of love and happiness.

Let my self-talk have a positive effect on me and others as well.

Thank you for listening to my prayer.

Seeker C: Other than practicing forgiveness, are there ways to make our self-talk positive?

Sirshree: Affirmations are an alternative too. You can program your subconscious mind by repeating positive thoughts such as:

- I am free from the negative self-talk of the past and am now rooted in peace.
- I have unquestionable faith in life and I am assured of my safety and wellbeing.
- I am peaceful, worthy and complete. I fully love and accept myself.
- I am worthy of being loved. I feel sublime and fresh. I lovingly take care of my body.
- I am soaking in the bliss of life and expressing it fully.
- I rest in full faith that all the right events and endeavors of my life are being scripted to perfection as per my divine plan.
- I am Consciousness. I am flowing freely and happily with my experiences in life. Everything is perfect.
- I rest in peace, having happily let go of my past.

- I am now living in the present. Blissful thoughts easily emerge within me.

- I am in good health, disease keeps away from me. I dwell in the bliss of perfect health and fitness.

The idea is to become aware of your negative self-talk and choose to repeat the affirmation that is the opposite of your negative self-talk. Again the practice of forgiveness itself is enough too. As you continue erasing old karmic lines of negative self-talk through the practice of forgiveness and keep improving your self-talk with awareness, you will witness miraculous transformations in your life. You will see all your negativity dissolving. You will usher in all good things like love, peace, health, positivity and prosperity into your life.

thirteen

Seeker B: Ever since I started practicing forgiveness, I've been feeling serene and peaceful. I found myself helping people much more. My co-worker was out this week and I put aside my own priorities to complete a project for him. I was happy to help him. I didn't expect any appreciation for that, but when my manager thanked him in front of all without mentioning me, I felt resentful. I decided to only focus on my work and not help anyone anymore.

Sirshree: Our tendencies, hardened habits and vices are hidden factors that produce karmic lines without our knowledge. After practicing forgiveness a little, we believe that we are free from them until we face situations like these, which trigger them. Here is an example.

A hermit performed penance for several years in the Himalayas after which, he became peaceful and stable. He remained in constant bliss and devotion. When he returned to his village, the villagers welcomed him with great respect and cheer. The hermit's face was glowing with splendor and peace. Everyone rushed to bow down before him to take his blessings. In the melee, one of the villagers accidentally stepped on his foot. Screaming in pain, he berated the man just like he would have before leaving for the Himalayas.

A lake accumulates garbage at the bottom. With time, the dirt settles and becomes invisible from the top, making the water appear clean and clear. It believes itself to be clean and free of garbage. It remains in this delusion until one day someone pokes a stick into it and agitates it. The garbage at the bottom comes to the surface and the water begins to appear muddy. The lake comes to know about its own dirt.

Seeker B: Does that mean the feeling of resentment was already within me and that this incident helped reveal it?

Sirshree: Yes. The garbage of tendencies, hardened habits and vices is accumulated within us over several years. Incidents in our life act like a stirrer to bring that garbage to surface. The garbage is reflected through our behavior and reactions. We knowingly or unknowingly perform wrong deeds.

As soon as someone disturbed the hermit, the garbage of anger and irritation, which had been suppressed within him, rose up to the surface. Even years of penance in the Himalayas hadn't cleansed it.

Seeker A: But how are tendencies and hardened habits formed in the first place?

Sirshree: First we create karmic lines through our thoughts and actions. When we repeatedly think or act in the same way, the corresponding karmic lines get ingrained as tendencies or hardened habits in our subconscious mind. These tendencies control us and make us draw new karmic lines, knowingly or unknowingly, from time to time. Karmic lines form tendencies and tendencies form further karmic lines and we get trapped in a vicious cycle. We don't even know how many karmic lines and tendencies are accumulated in our subconscious mind over the years until they get triggered by incidents, just like it happened with the hermit.

Here are a few more examples:

Suppose a child lies for the first time to avoid getting into trouble. He creates a karmic bondage for himself. He doesn't realize it and comes to believe that it's beneficial to lie and hence keeps repeating the behavior. As a consequence, a tendency of lying gets ingrained in his subconscious mind. Afterwards, the tendency controls him and he will end up attracting situations in his life that will make him lie even more. This leads to the formation of further karmic lines and reinforcement of that tendency. Some day or the other, he has to face the consequences of his actions. He may even face situations where people deceive him. And at that time, he fails to realize that his tendencies are today making him reap the consequences. Instead he complains to God, "Why me? Why are you doing this to me?"

Here is another example:

During the rainy season, streams flow freely down the hills. These streams follow the same pathways in every monsoon. Why? Because the ridges that are carved by the constant flow of water become more deeply ingrained each year. When the water was flowing initially, it took effort to clear the obstacles along the way. But later, these pathways provide least resistance. The pathways formed by the ridges represent tendencies and the flow of water along these pathways symbolizes behavior driven by habit.

Seeker C: But if tendencies take charge of us and unconsciously create further karmic lines, how can we be free from them?

Sirshree: (laughs) By performing the spiritual practice of forgiveness! If the hermit had identified his karmic line as soon as it surfaced, and erased it through the practice of forgiveness, he would have saved himself from creating a new karmic line.

Any changes in mood, memory, place, behavior, or even weather and other life events act as a stirrer to upset us from time to time. As soon as we get ruffled, our ingrained tendencies come to the surface and take control of us. It's up to us how we handle them and the associated karmic lines. Should we allow our tendencies to create new karmic lines? Or should we wipe our tendencies clean by practicing forgiveness? The choice is entirely ours.

If you have understood the secret of karmic lines, you will contemplate about your tendencies, hardened habits and vices and cleanse them using the tool of forgiveness. This way, your responses will have no trace of old tendencies and will not create new karmic lines.

Seeker B: But I still feel that my manager shouldn't have ignored my contribution. I feel like clarifying his misunderstanding.

Sirshree: You can do that. But as long as you believe that the cause of your problem lies in the outside world, you are going to create further karmic lines. You may feel that you have resolved the problem, but unknowingly you have invited more.

The incidents happening in your life today are a result of your past karmic lines and your present responses to those incidents are also driven by your past karmic lines.

Seeker C: This means that we are not living a fresh, new life. We are living the same old, stale life.

Sirshree: Yes, that's true. In reality, life is full of new and fresh present moments. But it's been overshadowed by past karmic lines. Past lines have burdened life to such an extent that life seems like nothing but problems. We feel pulled by difficulties and we live stressful lives with heavy hearts.

When you gain a firm conviction that your own karmic lines are causing problems, you will stop trying to solve them on the outside. Instead, you will work on them from inside by practicing forgiveness.

Always remember that responses that are new and fresh with awareness free you from the past and create a new life for you.

Seeker B: But how can I be alert at all times and practice forgiveness?

Sirshree: Whenever dormant karmic lines arise in your awareness, for any reason, always remember the mantra "*It has arisen to get erased.*" No matter what problems you have, don't be scared. Someone may insult you or be rude, some incident might make you sad, you may run into obstacles in life, you may lose your way, and so on. Whatever happens, always remember that it is raising its head to get erased. Be happy that your karmic account is getting settled and you are allowing God to cleanse you within.

With this mantra, when you accept parcels and practice forgiveness, your dormant karmic lines are erased. By responding with awareness, you will stop creating new karmic lines. Gradually, a time will come when all your old stock of karmic lines will be cleared and you will be completely cleansed from within.

Tendencies that don't come to light never get erased. They keep piling lines upon lines and burden you more and more. Therefore, investigate within yourself and honestly seek out hidden tendencies and vices. Accept them without hesitation. It takes courage to encounter your own hidden tendencies. Only when you do this will you be able to seek forgiveness for them.

To eliminate your tendencies, hardened habits and vices, pray:

Dear GoD,

I seek forgiveness for .... (your tendency, hardened habit or vice).

Please forgive me for those thoughts and actions that have strengthened this tendency or vice.

Please uproot this tendency or vice and the related thoughts.

Please cleanse me from within.

Please give me strength and courage to easily let go of this tendency or vice.

I am completely ready to let go of it.

I favor the truth, not this tendency or vice.

Thank you very much for freeing me.

Thank you. Thank you. Thank you.

Say this prayer regularly and relentlessly perform the spiritual practice of forgiveness. If you get rid of even one tendency or vice, countless associated karmic lines will be erased on their own. Bring all your tendencies, hardened habits and vices to your awareness and erase them with the eraser of forgiveness.

fourteen

Seeker B: I am in good terms with my brother. However, there was an incident that occurred eight years ago when he slapped me. Whenever I disagree with him, I am reminded of that incident and feel depressed.

Sirshree: Some karmic lines lie dormant within us for several years, like a coiled snake sleeping in a basket. When the snake charmer shakes the basket a bit, the snake immediately wakes up and raises its head. There are many such karmic lines that lie coiled deep within us. They remain in a dormant state until someone or something shakes them.

Normally, we remain unaware of these lines. But when nature shakes us a bit, in the form of changes in our mood, place, life events, or when someone comes into our life who evokes past memories, our dormant karmic lines wake up and raise their head. They fill our mind with negative thoughts and we relive the sorrow all over again. By thinking of the past incident and going through turbulent emotions again, we create new karmic lines for ourselves.

These karmic lines can be formed with our loved ones, friends, relatives or even strangers. In this case, your brother's misbehavior hurt you. You created a karmic line with him by harboring hatred for him. You overcame your feelings temporarily and the karmic line became dormant.

But deep within, the hatred was still there.

Now, whenever you have a difference of opinion with him, you are reminded of the past incident. Immediately your karmic line rises up and stands tall. You experience hurt and hatred all over again and thus create another karmic line. This is how dormant karmic lines work. They are very common in relationships like mother-in-law and daughter-in-law, husband-wife, parents-children, etc.

Seeker A: Can we cleanse these karmic lines with the practice of forgiveness?

Sirshree: Yes, you can. But some of these lines are so deep that one or two sessions of forgiveness will not be enough. You need to relentlessly practice forgiveness in order to get rid of them. Every time the snake rears its head, you need to erase the head through forgiveness. Gradually, the snake will weaken and dissolve.

Seeker C: But this way it will take a long time to cleanse all of them. Is there a way where we can practice forgiveness even when these lines are not activated?

Sirshree: Yes, there is. For this, you need to understand three rules, three steps and three meditation practices.

Seeker B: What are they?

Sirshree: First understand the three rules:

1. Honest thinking: Honestly recognize your feelings in their true form and accept them. Be truthful and deceit-free with yourself. While practicing these meditations, when you recall past incidents, mistakes that you or others committed at that time will come to the light of your awareness. Don't resist or disown them.

2. Courage: Incidents that you don't wish to recall will also come to your mind. Don't be in denial about the feelings that arise. Instead of avoiding and suppressing them within, courageously face them.

3. Clarity: Have clarity and understanding in your thoughts while practicing these meditations. Witness each incident completely from a detached and unbiased standpoint, backed by the clarity of understanding you have today.

Seeker C: What are the three steps?

Sirshree: Here are the three steps:

1. While practicing these meditations, recall some unpleasant past incidents in which you were directly involved.
2. Understand that whatever happened in the past was because of your 'level of understanding' at that time. You could not have reacted differently then.
3. After going through each unpleasant incident that you can remember, accept them in totality and forgive yourself and the others involved in them.

Seeker A: We are eager to know about the meditations.

Sirshree: In the first meditation, you forgive others:

1. Sit in a meditative posture with your eyes closed.
2. Visualize your parents. Perhaps they shouted at you or possibly even punished you when you were growing up. Perhaps you are still upset with them over one or several incidents. Bring each one of those incidents before your eyes, one by one. Tell them

that what they did was correct based on their understanding and knowledge at that time. Forgive them. Tell them in your mind, "I love you. I accept you. I respect you. I forgive you. Please forgive me as well."

3. Visualize your siblings. Maybe your brother or sister taunted you or insulted you when you were growing up. Maybe they said or did something very recently. Bring each incident before your eyes related to your siblings about which you carry a feeling of hurt or hatred and forgive them. If it helps, tell them mentally that whatever they did at that time was based on their understanding then. Accept the incident. Visualize hugging them affectionately or saying that you love them. Tell them that you forgive them and seek their forgiveness too.

4. Recall unpleasant incidents involving all your friends and relatives. You may be carrying a feeling of hurt or a grudge for feeling ill-treated by them. Forgive them. Understand that by forgiving them, you are becoming free from hatred, regardless of them.

5. Similarly, recall unpleasant incidents involving others besides your friends and relatives, such as your neighbors, teachers, etc. Perhaps, a doctor or a policeman said or did something that pained you. Forgive everyone just like you have in the above steps.

6. With your eyes closed, feel happiness within. Feel that one by one all the bondages within you are getting untangled. You are forgiving yourself and others as well. Whatever incidents happened in the past were perfect based on the understanding of all those who were involved at that time. But today, things are different. You have raised your understanding. You have let go of those incidents and associated feelings and become free from

the burden of past incidents. From here on, lead a life free from burden.

7. Slowly open your eyes.

Were you able to forgive others and yourself?

Seeker B: My brother has been helpful after that incident eight years ago. I've been holding onto the memories of that incident and forgot all the good things he did for me.

Sirshree: Forgiveness removes your past prejudices and enables you to consider people without bias. The practice brings to your awareness the goodness of others, which you were otherwise failing to see. By forgiving others you are doing a favor for yourself, not others. By harboring negative feelings like hatred, resentment, and envy, you harm yourself before harming anyone else. Do yourself a favor by forgiving others and getting rid of the feeling of hatred.

Seeker B: Thanks for the insight. I will forgive myself and my brother.

Seeker A: I could forgive everyone else but not me. I feel at some places I have unnecessarily blamed the other person. I feel guilty for my behavior.

Sirshree: That's what the second meditation is all about. It helps untangle the guilt and sadness you may be carrying within you. This practice helps you to accept and forgive yourself for everything that you knowingly or unknowingly did in the past. Here are the steps:

1. Sit in a meditative posture with your eyes closed.
2. Recall incidents from your childhood. See yourself as a child. See yourself crying. Hug that child and say to him or her, "I love you so much."

3. Recall a major incident in your childhood for which you carry guilt. Maybe you fought with your brother, sister or teacher. Maybe you said something horrible to your parents. Maybe you said or did something which hurt a friend. Tell yourself that whatever you did at that time was based on your understanding at that time. Recall that incident again, hug that child i.e. yourself and say, "I forgive you. You acted based on your understanding at that time. I love you. I accept you. I forgive you."

4. Look at another incident about which you are angry with yourself. Maybe you as a child stole something and this memory is troubling you today. Lovingly tell yourself, "You acted based on your understanding at that time. I forgive you."

5. Now recall all those things that you know you shouldn't have done during adolescence or up until recently. You may have done something, consumed something like alcohol, or got into something that you shouldn't have. These memories may be troubling you. Look at the incident and tell yourself lovingly, "I forgive you. I accept you the way you are. I love you."

6. With eyes closed, now visualize your body in front of a mirror. Look at your eyes, hair, nose, and other parts of the body. Tell yourself, "I completely accept you the way you are." Wholeheartedly accept your body, your height, your skin complexion, your deformities if any and your sicknesses. As you do this, you can gently caress your face and body and say to yourself, "I love you." You may practice this step with open eyes in front of a mirror too. Now, slowly open your eyes.

This meditation helps free you from the feelings of guilt, sadness and inferiority. Remember, only after forgiving yourself can you forgive everyone else. So, how did you feel?

Seeker A: I felt a wave of relief with this meditation.

Sirshree: That's good. So far you have forgiven others and yourself. Let's proceed with the third meditation to seek forgiveness from others for the karmic lines you have drawn with them in the past, knowingly or unknowingly.

1. Sit in a meditative posture with your eyes closed.
2. Recall all your relationships, especially friends and family. For convenience, recall them in the order of A to Z.
3. Think of those you can connect with the alphabets A to Z. A for aunt, for example. Recall all the unpleasant interactions that happened with all aunts in your life. How did you feel at that time? If you think you drew karmic lines with them, seek forgiveness from them. It is best to seek forgiveness face to face, but if you are not able to, do so at the mental level.
4. Similarly, think of those you can connect with the alphabet B – such as your brother or boss. Wholeheartedly seek forgiveness from them for anything hurtful that you believe you may have done or said to them. Move through the remaining letters. C may stand for cousins or colleagues, D may stand for your dad, E for Earth, F for friends, G for guru or grandparents, H for husband, I for yourself, M for mother, N for neighbors, T for teachers, U for uncle, W for wife and so on. Make your own list to include every one you have come in contact with.
5. Slowly open your eyes.

Seeker C: I couldn't recall one for each alphabet in this session.

Sirshree: It's not necessary to recall everyone in a single meditation session. As and when you recall people, you can forgive them at that time or later with closed eyes in subsequent sessions.

Seeker B: Going back to the first meditation, I'm able to forgive a colleague for his minor mistakes but unable to forgive his major ones. As a result, I keep seething within.

Sirshree: In such situations, ask yourself whether you want to punish your colleague or punish yourself by seething within? By holding on to grudges and resentment you harm none but yourself. By constantly thinking of the incident, you only punish yourself. Why do you want to punish yourself for something that the other person has apparently done? It's always better to forgive the other person.

Also, forgiving doesn't mean that you shouldn't say anything to the other person. You may talk to your colleague and guide him appropriately so as to avoid mistakes in the future. The important thing is to stay free from any antipathy towards him. In this way, you can train yourself to forgive people and also help change their behavior.

Seeker A: Sometimes, even after forgiving someone mentally, I feel hatred.

Sirshree: At such times, reiterate what you have understood about why forgiveness is the way to liberation. This will make it easier for you to address and let go of recurring hatred. Mentally forgive and seek forgiveness all over again. Seek forgiveness for considering him or her as a separate 'body'. Having done this exercise twice or thrice, you may feel the reduction in the intensity of what you were feeling. Also, it is important to focus on incidents one by one and mentally release them one after the other.

Seeker B: Thank you Sirshree. This has been just wonderful! I feel light and feel no more hatred for others or guilt for myself. It is marvelous to feel so light.

Sirshree: Excellent! But whenever you draw a karmic line with someone, remember to immediately carry out this exercise. You may practice it later at night. Karmic lines can be formed anywhere and at any time. Make sure you forgive yourself too from time to time as incidents occur.

The eraser of forgiveness will be a great reminder to practice forgiveness whenever incidents occur. Always keep the eraser of forgiveness handy with you as a reminder.

Seeker B: I am sorry, I did not understand. Are you speaking figuratively, Sirshree?

Sirshree: No, literally. Can one of you please fetch a whiteboard eraser?

Seeker C (after a few minutes): Here it is, Sirshree.

Sirshree (peeling off a little of the felt cloth from the eraser): Today, almost everyone uses a mobile phone. So why not stick the felt cloth that you see on a white board eraser to the back of your mobile phone? Your phone with the eraser will remind you to use the eraser of forgiveness whenever you see it.

Seeker B: Amazing reminder!

Sirshree: Don't worry about what others might think of you, looking at your phone. You should be more concerned about your practice of forgiveness. Focus on erasing your karmic lines rather than worry about what others might think. Can you think of any other means of reminders?

Seeker C: I can change the wallpaper on my cell phone to remind me.

Seeker A: I fume a lot, especially when I am driving. I can actually paste a white board eraser on my dashboard.

Sirshree: Very good. All reminders are useful. Stick something above your bed if it reminds you to erase all lines that day before you go to sleep. With practice, you will be able to do so without any reminders.

fifteen

Seeker A: I can forgive everyone else except my mother-in-law. She hurt me so badly.

Sirshree: Some people practice forgiveness, but with conditions. They are able to forgive everyone, barring one or two individuals who seemingly hurt them deeply. It's true that in some situations there is so much hurt experienced, that it's not easy to forgive. But it's not impossible either. Your ability to forgive depends on your desire and readiness to achieve complete freedom. If this is indeed your aim, you will have to practice forgiveness one hundred percent.

If you look at Lord Rama's life in the Indian epic Ramayana, he practiced one hundred percent forgiveness while fulfilling his responsibilities. Even after his stepmother, Queen Kaikeyi, was instrumental in his exile from the kingdom on the eve of his coronation, he didn't create any karmic lines with her. Neither did he create karmic lines with the demons whom he vanquished. When he shot down the brutal demoness Taraka and she was breathing her last, he sought her forgiveness because he was duty bound to kill her. He hadn't killed her out of hatred and yet he asked for forgiveness.

If you feel hatred for someone, it indicates that there is some shortcoming in your perspective. You are not able to see the presence of God inside that person. Remind yourself of the understanding you have gained about karmic lines and forgiveness, and set your perspective right.

Seeker A: I tried practicing forgiveness with my mother-in-law, but somehow I am not able to. I feel I cannot forgive her for seven lifetimes.

Sirshree: When you forgive everyone except one person, even if you wish to, understand that this is that snake in the game of snakes and ladders that is not letting you reach the summit. Without erasing this snake, you can't reach the summit and attain a state of complete freedom. The snake could be a single karmic line, but bondage is after all bondage. There is no way to escape it. You will have to face it or risk creating new karmic lines because of it. If you think that you will not forgive your mother-in-law for seven lifetimes, you are trapped by the snake for long.

Now ask yourself which of the two you desire more and which is more important to you: attaining a state of complete freedom by reaching the summit or harboring hatred in your heart for your mother-in-law? Honestly contemplate: What have you achieved so far by nurturing hatred? Does your hatred harm your mother-in-law in any way? You will realize that hatred caused more harm to you than her. You waste your energy, your thoughts get polluted, and most importantly, you gamble with your freedom.

To erase such deep karmic lines pray to GoD and clearly state what you are in favor of:

Dear GoD,

I favor love, not hatred.

I favor complete freedom, not bondage.

Please give me the strength to practice

one hundred percent forgiveness.

After that, whenever you have thoughts of hatred in your mind, seek forgiveness for both of you.

Seeker C: How can we forgive criminals and terrorists who commit heinous crimes such as bombings and mass killings? Nobody would wish to forgive such people.

Sirshree: This example might help you.

Your computer has state-of-the-art technology, but operates based on the software loaded on it. If it gets infected with some harmful virus, it will not only harm your computer but also harm the other computers connected to the network. Now what will you do? Will you destroy your computer as it seems to be the root cause of all your technology problems? No, you will simply remove the virus from the computer and perhaps reformat the hard disk. If the problem persists, you might consult a specialist, but you won't blame the computer. Rather than destroying the computer, you will cleanse it inside and bring it back to normal operations.

The human body is but a machine. The thought process that runs the machine decides what that body will do. In case of criminals and terrorists, their way of thinking is the real culprit. This is why many Self-realized saints have taught to detest the sin but not the sinner. Their thought process can be changed by listening to truth, reading spiritual books, contemplation and staying in the company of truth seekers. Forgive them for their mindset and sinful tendencies. You are not asked to forgive them, but you are asked to cleanse them. Your prayers can cleanse their collective consciousness and positively impact their sinful tendencies. Pray to GoD:

Dear GoD,

Please cleanse them from within.

Please eradicate their sinful tendencies.

I seek forgiveness on their behalf.

Please forgive them and also forgive me as this is happening in my field of awareness.

Let these people too receive wisdom.

Let their understanding and consciousness rise.

Bestow upon them the same grace that you have bestowed upon me.

Please make them worthy enough to receive your grace.

Seeker C: But do they really change?

Sirshree: Everything impacts the collective consciousness. Ancient stories and mythologies hint at this:

Lord Buddha bestowed love, compassion and forgiveness upon the ruthless serial killer Angulimala and transformed him into a peaceful monk.

Similarly, the sage Narada imparted wisdom to the cruel hunter and fearless thief Ratnakara and made him contemplate. As a result, Ratnakara transformed into sage Valmiki.

Jesus did a similar thing. People inflicted severe pain on him through the ordeal leading to his crucifixion. But he prayed to God, "Please forgive them, for they know not what they do." If those people didn't even know that they were doing something wrong, how would they seek forgiveness? This is why Jesus sought forgiveness on their behalf. This is one hundred percent forgiveness, unconditional and unflinching.

And it is not just ancient stories alone. History is witness to transformational power of love and forgiveness.

In his last conquest of Kalinga, King Ashoka witnessed the massacre of thousands of soldiers on both sides of the battlefield. It is believed that he was overcome by remorse at the death and destruction he had caused. This led him to renounce violence and surrender to the teachings of Lord Buddha. Later, all that he did was for the wellbeing and spiritual progress of people. This earned him the title "Ashoka the Great". His name is forever linked with Lord Buddha in the pages of history.

More recently, the notorious dacoits of Chambal surrendered their arms after coming in contact with various saints. Freeing themselves from their sinful habits, they started leading a normal life.

Can you think of other examples?

Seeker B: Yes. I read recently that The Truth and Reconciliation Commission in South Africa has helped heal the injustices of the apartheid era to some extent. Also, Lynnie McTaggart has written a book titled "The Intention Experiment" which documents how the power of thoughts and prayers changes the world.

Sirshree: Good, you will find many more examples if you go out and seek them. The idea is simple: for your spiritual growth and for the benefit of the world, seek forgiveness on behalf of everyone, whether they are friends or foes, Samaritans or sinners, insiders or outsiders. If you continue to feel that you cannot forgive this one person for something he or she has committed, then you aren't practicing one hundred percent forgiveness.

Seeker C: There are so many sinners in the world. So, are those many people needed to seek forgiveness for them?

Sirshree: Those who are awakened and aware should seek forgiveness for those who are not aware. If you cannot forgive them, you can at least ask GoD to forgive them.

Understand this through a story.

Many beautiful flowers blossomed in a garden. A hunter was passing by and was mesmerized by their beauty. He plucked a lot of flowers and laughingly went away leaving the garden almost barren. A virtuous, saintly person was watching this scene and felt sad looking at the state of the garden. He too was taken in by the beauty of the flowers. He thought, "The garden is almost destroyed now. Since there are only a few flowers left, why not pluck them to offer to God?" Accordingly, he plucked a couple of flowers. Suddenly, the God of the Garden appeared before him and started rebuking him. "I will curse you for your impudence", the deity said. The saint lamented and apologized, "I am not the sole cause of this destruction. A hunter was here before me and he destroyed the garden. I just took couple of flowers."

The deity replied, "I know you didn't do this entirely."

The man was taken aback, "If you knew everything, then why didn't you curse the hunter? He destroyed the entire garden. I just picked few flowers."

The God of the garden replied, "He was a cruel hunter. How can I expect him to care for plants when he is desensitized to humans and animals and kills them for his selfish ends? He has a very low level of consciousness. But you are a sensitive and saintly gentleman. I expect you to help restore the garden instead of destroying it further. Imagine if you'd let the few flowers live on, they would give birth to new flowers to make the garden beautiful again."

Hearing this, the saint realized his mistake and sought forgiveness for his action.

Those who are awake and whose level of consciousness has risen are responsible for practicing forgiveness. Only they can have a non-individualistic, selfless outlook and can look out for the well-being of others.

sixteen

Seeker C: In addition to terrorism, the world is grappling with problems such as poverty, unemployment, recession, corruption, disease, famine and so on. Some people directly cause them and some others indirectly add fuel to the fire by engaging in negative self-talk and spread anger, hatred, sorrow and bitterness regarding these issues. How can we carry the burden of their wrong-doings?

Sirshree: You don't have to carry the burden of their wrong-doings outwardly. Take responsibility inwardly. Again, don't forgive them, cleanse them. Understand that the world is like a big home. Whatever is going on in the world is a combined effect of every inhabitant's feelings, thoughts, words and actions.

Here is a story to understand it better:

There was a king who was very particular about justice. No crime, big or small, would go unpunished in his Kingdom. The king would give the harshest punishment to criminals to dissuade others from crime. Once, a person killed his neighbor in a unique way. He made a sharp weapon out of ice and hoped that when the ice melted, the evidence would vanish. But the king's men were competent enough to find this.

The king sentenced the man to death by hanging. Preparations were made at the center of a busy public place. A saint, whom the king revered, saw what was happening. Looking at the condition of the murderer, he felt pity for him. He went to the king and asked him the reason for the punishment. "Your Holiness, this man is a murderer. He has killed his neighbor, so I have sentenced him to death."

The saint said, "It is true that the final act of crime was committed by this person. But he is not the only culprit. Everyone in this kingdom including you, Your Highness, is involved in this crime." The king was taken aback by this accusation. He said, "How can it be, Your Holiness?"

The saint approached the murderer and asked, "Son, why did you kill your neighbor?"

The man replied, "I didn't intend to kill him. He was my friend. But on that day, I heard his wife screaming and crying. He was beating his wife and I couldn't tolerate this and killed him."

The saint asked further, "Was his wife a relative?"

"No, Your Holiness. As a child, I saw my father beating my mother. As I was small, I couldn't do anything. But those incidents made me angry. When I heard the woman next door screaming and crying, I saw my mother in her, and my father in my friend. All my pent-up anger came out and I killed him."

The saint looked at the king and said, "You see, Your Highness, his father is equally guilty. And everyone who made his father that way is also guilty."

The saint asked, "You committed the murder in a fit of rage. Where did you get the weapon made of ice?"

"I had read a book about unusual weapons and methods of killing. I had made the weapon just to see whether it worked. I was going to use it on an animal to experiment. It so happened that just when I had finished making the weapon with ice, that I heard my neighbor's wife's cries."

The saint said to the king, "Your Highness, the author of the book, its publisher and its seller are also responsible for the crime. They inspired this man to make a deadly weapon."

He further asked the man, *"You were in a fit of rage and had a weapon, but God has also given you the power of discrimination to differentiate between right and wrong. Couldn't you have exercised control over yourself?"*

The man replied, *"I wasn't thinking clearly because I was drunk."*

"So you also drink regularly?"

"No, not regularly. But on that day my friend forced me to."

The saint said to the king, "See? His friend has also contributed to the murder."

The friend was summoned and asked, "Why did you force him to drink?"

The friend replied, *"A new liquor store opened next to my house. They were offering huge discounts. That's why I bought a lot of liquor and forced my friend to join me."*

Then the shopkeeper was called for. He revealed that he could offer big discounts because the government had slashed taxes on a range of commodities that included liquor. When the officials were asked why, they revealed that the king himself had ordered tax cuts on liquor because of excessive production that year.

The king explained, *"Our kingdom is the leading manufacturer of liquor. We even export to neighboring kingdoms. We earn a lot of money from these exports and use the money for the development of our people."*

The saint said, *"But Your Highness, liquor played an important role in this murder. If you want to stop such crimes, you need to stop sale of this poison that dulls man's power of reasoning."*

The king replied, *"But this is not possible. How will I take care of the expenses? Our treasury will be depleted in no time."*

Others also joined in and said, "No, no. This is impossible. Banning liquor will affect our revenue and standard of living."

The saint said, "If you don't have the courage to ban liquor, at least have the courage to accept the fact that all of you are responsible for the murder to some extent and in some form. Your thoughts and actions have influenced this man to commit the murder, in some way or the other. Today he is being punished. Tomorrow, you may face the consequences."

This is also our story. We are all part of the world and are responsible for the situation that has arisen today. Each one of us is contributing to it, directly or indirectly. If you are not directly involved, at least stop the negative self-talk and hatred, resentment and any disregard towards your responsibilities. Understand that whatever you passionately think, feel or describe turns into reality. This is also a negative contribution toward the problems in the world.

Seeker C: Can we practice forgiveness in this situation to eliminate our contributions?

Sirshree: Yes, you can. Have you ever made or seen a house of cards? Children play the game of making a house of cards by placing playing cards one on top of the other in triangular formation. If you remove even one card from the formation, the whole house of cards begins to tumble down. Problems of the world are like this. Everyone has contributed a card each to this house. Every negative thought about the world is akin to a card. Your contribution might be very small, perhaps only 0.00001%.

But if you practice forgiveness for this infinitesimal contribution, the problems in the world will begin to be eliminated. The house of cards will begin to eliminate. It is a huge deck that has been built over the years. But it can indeed collapse and all problems can be solved. This may seem far-fetched, but it isn't. Your little prayer can lead to a great revolution in the world. This is no less than a miracle.

Whenever you see problems at home, in your community, in the country or in the world, pray to GoD:

Dear GoD,

I am sorry.

Please forgive me for whatever negative contribution I have made to this problem.

Make a positive contribution through creative and good thoughts. If everyone does this, negativity will give way to positivity.

Seeker C: Yes, I will do this. This way, even wars can be resolved. Today, if military forces fight with each other out of hatred, the hatred provokes more hatred and sows the seeds of the next war. But if the military officials practice forgiveness before matters escalate, the dispute can be resolved.

Sirshree: True! Love augments love. If everyone in the world understands this secret, miracles will begin to happen. A world of love, joy and peace can be established. As the level of consciousness rises, you become free from hatred, resentment, greed and attachment. Whatever you do, it will be with the selfless feeling of responsibility.

Seeker C: As part of my positive contribution toward the world, I feel like praying to God:

Dear God,

Please uplift everyone.

Please forgive everyone.

Please keep an eye on everyone and their wellbeing.

Sirshree: It's a good resolution. And remember, what God stands for. You can join in the world peace prayer at the foundation which tens of thousands of people perform at 9:09 a.m. or p.m. every day.

Seeker B: I am aware of this initiative by Tejgyan Global Foundation and I do join in either at 9.09 in the evening or morning. Even if I am traveling outside of India, I make it a point to pray at this time corresponding to the time in India so that I can join thousands of others at the same time.

Seeker C: What exactly happens when so many people pray at the same time?

Sirshree: In this prayer, you send positive thoughts to the entire world. You desire love, joy and peace for the globe. When lots of people pray in this manner at the same time from wherever they are, countless positive thoughts are created. This can collectively raise Earth's level of consciousness and helps resolve problems and dissolve negativity. Whether or not your prayers reach others in the world, when you pray for others with a selfless feeling, you become receptive to the divine grace that is being showered on the globe.

Offer the following prayer by visualizing that the divine grace is being bestowed on this world. Let's all pray now without worrying about what time it is:

Visualize that divine white light is being showered upon Earth.

Higher Consciousness in the form of golden light is emanating from Earth.

All negativity in the world is being eliminated.

Every being is opening up for love, bliss, peace and forgiveness.

Everyone is being forgiven.

Everyone is able to forgive themselves and others.

Everyone is being cleansed within.

Everyone is becoming receptive to divine grace.

seventeen

Seeker C: What is the actual impact of holding onto karmic lines like hatred and anger?

Sirshree: Besides hampering your spiritual growth and mental wellbeing, karmic lines impact you physically too.

Seeker B: Oh! I can't understand this connection. How can karmic lines, which are mental in nature, lead to physical diseases?

Sirshree: To understand this in detail, let's first understand some fundamentals about the body.

If you watch your body and its organs as a detached witness, you will be able to view the truth of the human body-mind mechanism – it is merely a machine! The way several mechanical components come together to form a big machine, similarly, several organs and parts come together to create the human body. Every part of our body performs some specific function and all parts together create a great machine. Our body is at our service twenty-four hours a day from birth to death. It helps express the divine qualities of the Self.

The body is designed in such a way that it regenerates every seven years. Stem-cell biologists have proven that most of the body's tissues are under constant renewal and the average age of all the cells in an adult's body is about 7 to 10 years. That means you may believe your body to be 45 years old, for example, but your body cells are only around 7 years young. Cells are constantly dividing, regenerating and dying. By nature, the body is designed to be disease-free.

Then why do diseases occur? The root cause is that we have assumed ourselves to be limited individual body-mind mechanisms, which are separate from the Universal pure Consciousness. We have created a false idea of our identity. We assume a false idea of who we are, based on the belief systems inherited from childhood and from our upbringing. As a result, we become disconnected from our essential healthy nature. This reflects at the mental level in the form of emotional clutter, defeatist tendencies, intellectual clouding and lack of vitality. This, in turn, causes impairment and imbalance in our physiology. This is the seed of disease.

You might ask, even if diseases do occur, why do they linger if our tissues are being completely regenerated over time? The answer lies in karmic lines. The mind gets infected with defilements such as anger, hatred, resentment, guilt, self-doubt, fear, ill-will, jealousy, etc. Our body is the mind's mirror. Each of our thoughts, beliefs, assumptions and feelings create karmic lines that are stored in our cellular memory. New cells inherit these karmic memories from parent cells. The effect of the disease continues in our bodies, affecting their functioning and their health in turn. This explains the continuation of chronic diseases like asthma, hypertension, gastric ulcers and cancer that linger for many years. Every karmic line formed due to our thoughts, feelings, speech and actions can potentially cause disease.

Seeker B: Can we cure physical diseases with the practice of forgiveness?

Sirshree: Yes, you can certainly impact your physical health positively through forgiveness. You can seek forgiveness from the diseased body part or organ and promise to take care of it. The various parts and organs of your body are conscious entities in their own right. They gain strength when you apologize to them, love them and thank them. When they gain strength, they eliminate illnesses on their own.

Seeker C: Am still finding it difficult to understand how forgiveness can bring about changes in our physical wellbeing?

Sirshree: It is the most obvious truth that thoughts influence our body. When you get the thought of raising your hand, it triggers neurons in your brain to execute movements of your hand muscles in a coordinated manner so as to raise it. All physical actions through our bodies are actually wondrous examples of how thoughts regulate the body. However, most medical practitioners, until recently, have not considered mental factors while diagnosing disease. Their primary focus is on biochemical aspects. They attempt to treat disease by effecting chemical changes in the body.

There is unquestionable scientific evidence that has proven beyond doubt that our thoughts are largely influential in determining our physical wellbeing.

In a groundbreaking experiment, Dr. Masaru Emoto and his associates from Japan exposed water samples from various sources to a variety of spoken words – both positive and negative expressions. They also exposed water samples to a variety of music – both harmonious and jarring. Subsequently, they froze the water samples and photographed the crystals that were formed in frozen water.

Water samples exposed to words like "Love you", 'Peace', and "Thank You" formed beautiful hexagonal crystals. However, water samples exposed to words like 'Fool' or "Hate you", "You make me sick" produced malformed and fragmented crystals. This experiment provided concrete visual evidence of how water reacted to both positive and negative energy.

Do you know what the major constituent of the human body is?

Seeker C: Water! The average human body is made of 70 percent water.

Sirshree: Exactly! Throughout our physical lifetime, our bodies exist mostly as water. Since we are made primarily of water and since water can be influenced by positive and negative energy, it becomes all the more vital that we work on our thoughts and feelings. Our inner self-talk can directly impact our whole being including physical health.

Seeker C: Wow! I had never considered this. This is indeed a revelation!

Seeker A: Are there any other evidences that prove the dominance of mind over matter.

Sirshree: You might have heard of people becoming healed after taking a sugar pill or following a procedure that convinces them of wellbeing. This is a common phenomenon, which is known as the placebo effect. It is a direct result of your mind believing that you will get better even if the treatment was faked.

The placebo response is one of the most fascinating manifestations of the body's self-healing capabilities. It is the result of partnership between a mind that believes in the effectiveness of a given treatment and the body that fulfills the expectations of the mind by exercising its inbuilt healing intelligence.

Also, there are cases reported of people suddenly getting healed from cancer and other terminal illnesses, merely because they have had a profound change in their beliefs or outlook towards life. Such cases are known as spontaneous remission.

There is also research conducted in Russia that proves that the human DNA contains encoded data that follows the same grammar rules of syntax and semantics as our human languages. The evolution of human languages is not a coincidence, but rather a reflection of our inherent DNA. Due to this, human DNA resonates with human language. So it turns out that we can use words and sentences of human language to influence living DNA! This has been experimentally proven. DNA present in living tissue responds to language-modulated inputs.

This scientifically explains why affirmations and autosuggestions have such strong effects on our bodies and physiology. Thus, when you focus your conscious attention on any specific body organ or physiological process and communicate in words, they respond to you. If you seek forgiveness from any body part, it has the potential of releasing pent-up cellular memories and restoring the healthy blueprint.

Seeker B: This is fantastic! Does this mean that the practice of forgiveness, in itself, is enough to heal the physical body?

Sirshree: No. This does not imply that you should solely rely on the practice of forgiveness or positive self-talk alone, to cure physical ailments. Any attempt to diagnose and treat an illness should be done under the direction of a certified physician or healthcare professional. Follow their recommendations in addition to the practice of forgiveness.

Seeker A: How do I practice forgiveness to heal a physical ailment?

Sirshree: The following forgiveness prayer is for healing ailing body parts and erasing related karmic lines.

Invite: *Dear divine form of.......... (name the ailing body part, organ), I invite you into my field of awareness.*

Seek forgiveness: *With God (or guru or any source of inspiration) as my witness, I seek your forgiveness.*

I failed to pay attention to you all these years. You have suffered a lot. Please forgive me for my carelessness and ignorance. I love you. From now on, I will take care of you. I will never do anything that causes you trouble. I am grateful to you for your unconditional love and support. Thank you.

You have the power to heal yourself. There is no disease in the world that you can't cure. God's divine power is constantly at your disposal. Please begin to heal yourself now. Please continue to heal yourself even after leaving my field of awareness. I expect health miracles.

Express gratitude: *Thank you very much for being in my field of awareness, forgiving me and healing yourself. I love you and respect you. Thank you. Thank you. Thank you.*

This prayer will give strength to the ailing body parts. They will start responding to medicines and the ailment will vanish. If you have any health issues, express your love and respect to the ailing body part whenever you remember. This will raise your level of consciousness and you will realize that your body parts can listen, feel and respond to your emotions and intentions. Regularly practice forgiveness with your body. You will be surprised to see your health improve.

Seeker A: I really feel thankful to my body. It's supporting me so well.

Sirshree: Yes, be grateful as it is supporting you every moment. Thank those body parts and organs that are healthy and in good condition. Seek forgiveness from them:

Dear .... (name of the body part, organ),
I haven't thanked you enough for your unending support.
I am sorry for misusing you; please forgive me.
Please continue functioning as efficiently as you have always been.
Thank you. Thank you. Thank you.

Express gratitude to your body parts for working efficiently all these years. Pray to them and ask them to continue working efficiently for the years to come. When you perform the spiritual practice of forgiveness with people at bedtime, do the same with your body as well. Lovingly speak to your body and use the magic mantras of Accept, Forgive and Let-go. This will erase the karmic lines you have drawn. You will feel relieved and your physical and mental health will improve.

SECTION III

Clearing Deeper Impressions

eighteen

Seeker C: Ever since I started practicing forgiveness, I'm feeling less stressed and more relaxed. I am enjoying my life. It's not that I don't have any problems but I'm finding this state so beautiful! I'm curious, what has been exactly happening in my life since I began imbibing the spiritual practice?

Sirshree: When we start practicing forgiveness, we become sensitive towards our frail and thin karmic lines. As soon as we hurt anyone, knowingly or unknowingly, through our thoughts, feelings, speech and actions, we immediately practice forgiveness and promise not to repeat the mistake again. This way, we cleanse ourselves at the surface level.

As your understanding and awareness increases, you delve deeper and erase your past dormant karmic lines that were lying coiled like snakes. A deeper cleansing has begun. You forgave those people whom you found impossible to forgive. You broke thicker and heavier bondages of karma. Your stress level has lightened and you are finding it easy to open up, blossom and enjoy in life.

Some people are content with just this much progress. But those who wish to attain complete liberation investigate deeper within. Through contemplation they examine their subconscious mind where past dormant karmic lines lurk. These are akin to dangerous snakes with thousands of heads. These snakes are associated with our core thoughts, our DNA, karmic lines passed onto us by our ancestors, and our injured memories from our past.

So, what do you want to do? Go deeper or stop where you are?

Seeker C: I want to delve deeper. I want to attain complete liberation from all karmic lines.

Sirshree: You began by saying you still have some problems. What kind of problem are you referring to?

Seeker C: I still have money problems. My social relations are not harmonious and I'm very short-tempered.

Sirshree: What are your beliefs about money?

Seeker C: I believe that money is the root cause of all problems in life.

Sirshree: What makes you believe so?

Seeker C: As a child, I saw my father squabbling with my uncle over money. My mother told me that the root cause of their conflict was money and money could turn even brothers into enemies. Later on, I witnessed something similar with my close friend. His family broke apart due to conflicts over their property. Recently, I watched a movie where the main character deceived his best friend for money, and the friend sought revenge later. All the things I've seen throughout my life have convinced me that money is the root cause of all problems.

Sirshree: Your financial problems are because of this core thought that money is the root cause of all problems in life. You have nurtured this core thought since your childhood and believed it to be true. Because of your faith in this core thought, you get evidences that reinforce this belief. As long as you hold onto this core thought, you will face money problems and you will not find harmony in your relationships.

Consider an example:

After a long tiring day, you go to bed at midnight. In the dim light of the bedroom, you suddenly spot a snake in your bed and scream loudly. Someone rushes to your room and flicks on the light. In the bright light, you see a rope in place of the snake. You realize that what you thought was a snake is actually just a rope. You're relieved and your stress vanishes in a moment.

What turned the rope into a snake? Your core thought, your strong belief. Such thoughts are like lines engraved on stone. These core thoughts or beliefs have become the foundation of your personality; they define you. Thus, getting rid of these core thoughts seems to shake your definition of who-you-are. Hence, you've never paid attention to them. In order to erase these deeply rooted karmic lines, you need to understand and recognize these core thoughts.

Seeker C: Do you mean to say that I am facing problems in my life because of my strong belief that money is the root cause of all problems?

Sirshree: Yes. *Whatever you believe, manifests in your life.* If money were the root cause of all problems, then you would find all the wealthy people of the world steeped in problems. But this is certainly not the case. There are many who enjoy their wealth and lead a smooth life. The real problem lies with the core belief that is ingrained in your subconscious mind. As long as you hold onto this belief, you will continue to experience situations in life as problems caused by money. And these experiences only reinforce your belief.

Here is another example to understand this:

A mother didn't allow her child to have street food. She warned him, "If you eat street food, you'll suffer from diarrhea." The child was upset and thought, "All my friends eat street food. They don't get diarrhea, so why would I?" One day, he ate his favorite street food without his mother's knowledge. While he ate, he constantly thought of his mother's warning. Due to his negative thought, he got a bout of diarrhea. When his mother came to know, she scolded him, "Didn't I warn you that street food results in diarrhea? Do you believe me now?" She transferred her core thought to her son, which troubled him throughout his life.

This example doesn't mean that all street food is good for health. Discern with an open mind what food is healthy for you.

Seeker A: (laughing) Can you please provide other examples of core thoughts?

Sirshree: Every person has different core thoughts. They could be related to money, relationships, health, success, business, work, friendship, love, freedom, and many others.

Some common core thoughts are…

- It is difficult for me to save money.
- Life is difficult.
- Marriages, where the partners choose each other, usually fail.
- I never get anything in life with ease.
- The world is filled with dishonest people.
- Goodness has no value in today's world.
- I am always sick with some ailment or other.
- I don't deserve the best in life.

One core thought is like a snake with a thousand heads. This is not one karmic line but a whole bundle of lines. It is a knot of millions of thoughts. If you untie this one knot, the whole bundle will untangle at once and a thorough cleansing will happen from within.

Seeker B: How can we identify core thoughts within us?

Sirshree: Nature has created everything in abundance for everyone. If it's not reaching you, or not reaching you in the right form, then somewhere your own thoughts are posing hurdles. In ignorance, you are giving strength to your hurdles.

First contemplate deep within to dig out the core thoughts lying within you. Whatever problems are recurring in your life, identify the thoughts working behind them. You will start noticing a pattern. That is a core thought. Understand that they are fake and wrong. They have no power of their own. You only give them strength by blindly believing in them.

Seeker A: How can we get rid of them?

Sirshree: You can erase them with the practice of forgiveness. Pray to GoD:

Dear GoD,

Please forgive me.

Please erase my limiting core thoughts from my mind.

Please cleanse me thoroughly.

Thank you. Thank you. Thank you.

You can also add, "Please erase the thought that money is the root cause of all evil from my mind." You can seek forgiveness for harboring this thought. When you have time to contemplate deeply, try to identify each one of your core thoughts. Seek forgiveness for each and every one. This will propel you towards liberation.

Either join your hands or open them outwards. Find any posture that draws you into the feeling of prayer. Then release your pent-up feelings. From the bottom of your heart, seek forgiveness for yourself and for others.

Dear GoD,

I seek your forgiveness.

Please forgive me for my ignorance and semi-unconsciousness.

Please liberate me from the core thought of ....
(specify the core thought)

Please forgive me for all related wrong core thoughts.

In ignorance, I held them as the truth,
but in reality, they had no trace of truth.

I am sorry for this.

I accept full responsibility for my mistake.

Please forgive me. Please cleanse me from within.

Erase all my karmic lines, and let not a single one remain within me.

You have the power to erase my lines and cleanse me from within.

Please do so.

My ignorance and core thoughts also affected others.

Please forgive me for that.

I seek your forgiveness from the bottom of my heart.

Please forgive everyone. Please cleanse everyone.

Thank you. Thank you. Thank you.

Seeker B: What exactly happens after we practice forgiveness?

Sirshree: With regular practice of forgiveness, the knot of your bundle of karmic lines will open. The snake with thousands of heads will be eliminated in one blow.

When core thoughts are erased, you will see money flowing, relationships improving, health blossoming, joy at the workplace, and smoothness in every facet of your life. Everything will flow like a song for you, whether you're alone or among people. This is the magic of forgiveness.

nineteen

Seeker C: My mother says that I am short tempered, just like my grandfather. She keeps saying that my grandfather may have been reborn in my form. Can this be true? I don't understand how my short temper is related to my grandfather.

Sirshree: Consider that it could be the effect of karmic lines passed down from ancestors through genes.

Seeker C: I'm confused.

Sirshree: Understand this with an example:

A grandfather named Purvatilal, his son Muktiprasad, and his grandson Kishorilal used to live together. Due to poor eyesight, Purvatilal couldn't see anything without glasses. He always meant to put his glasses on immediately after waking up in the morning, but he was forgetful by nature. He never remembered and always bumped into the furniture in the house.

In order to overcome his shortcoming, he stuck a note on his back before going to bed. The note read, "Pinch me to remind me about wearing my glasses." It was his heartfelt prayer to God. However, the note slipped off while he was asleep. When he woke, he forgot about everything as usual.

Later Kishorilal came and took a nap in his grandfather's bed. When he got up, the note stuck to his back without his knowing.

As he worked, everyone read the note on his back. They pinched him and reminded him to wear his glasses. Kishorilal was bewildered, "I have reading glasses. Why should I wear them now? And why don't you mind your own business? Whether I wear them or not is my choice."

As he was completely unaware of the note on his back, he was irritated with all the pinching and taunting and rebuked in return. He wondered, "Why does everyone behave with me like this?"

He gathered his patience and asked someone, "Brother, tell me, how does it concern you whether I wear my glasses or not?" The man replied, "You have stuck a note on your back, asking people to pinch you and remind you to wear your glasses!" Kishorilal realized that the fault was with the note that was stuck onto him, not the people. He was the cause of his problems, albeit unknowingly.

In this example, we are Kishorilal. We are unsuspectingly carrying the karmic lines passed onto us by our ancestors through our genes. We fail to understand why certain incidents are happening in our life and complain, "Why is this happening to me?"

Seeker B: What do these inherited karmic lines consist of?

Sirshree: The karmic lines inherited through our genes could be in the form of our ancestors' habits, tendencies, karmic bondages, ailments, virtues and vices.

Seeker C: How do they impact us?

Sirshree: The genetic blueprint in our cells and the traits inherited through our genes decide our physical and mental constitution. But not every generation will have the same traits passed down through their genes. Sometimes, they may skip a generation or more. Just like what happened with Muktiprasad. He didn't get the trait of forgetfulness from his father but Kishorilal did.

Again, it's not mandatory that it will always happen in every alternate generation. It's a permutation and combination of our ancestors' habits, tendencies, karmic bondages, ailments, virtues and vices. When we fail to understand these inherited traits, we believe that an ancestor has taken birth again – just as your mother keeps telling you.

Seeker A: Do karmic lines inherited through our genes prove to be the cause of our downfall?

Sirshree: If you grumble in your mind or fight with people due to the suffering caused by these karmic lines, you create new lines that will haunt you in the future. It will also create new parcels which nature will deliver to you in due course. The vicious cycle of creating new karmic lines and creating suffering will go on continuously.

Let's continue with our example:

After growing up, Kishorilal was married to Leelavati. Their match was made after a lot of scrutiny and study by the Hindu tradition. Their horoscopes and palm lines were checked for compatibility. Only after a thorough evaluation was the match approved. But no one was aware of their karmic lines.

How was the relationship between Kishorilal and Leelavati? Their marriage was not at all smooth. Every day, Leelavati would remind Kishorilal to buy household items and he would forget. She would flare up when he returned empty handed. They constantly bickered and argued with each other. Kishorilal didn't know that he had inherited the trait of forgetfulness through his genes and, in accordance with his prayer, his wife was helping him to remember. Instead, he felt hurt by her behavior and rebuked her. For her part, Leelavati didn't bother to consider that Kishorilal would be tired after a day's work and may have forgotten to buy the items. The harmony in their house was often disrupted.

Seeker A: I never thought that karmic lines passed through our genes can cause this. I took it as part and parcel of life. How can we get out of this vicious cycle?

Sirshree: We attract those people in our lives who deliver karmic parcels to us and help us settle our karmic accounts. Relationships are meant for liberating us from our karmic lines. But for this to happen, we need to raise our awareness and level of understanding. Failing this, we continue to create even more lines.

If Kishorilal and Leelavati had accepted their mistakes and sought forgiveness from each other, they would have been happy with their situation. They would have helped each other to be free from their karmic lines.

They are only examples. The same thing is happening everywhere in every relationship: spouses, siblings, friends, neighbors, colleagues and even nations. Many people, instead of apologizing, are busy pointing out others' faults and trying to prove them guilty.

The vicious cycle of suffering and new karmic lines can be turned around, just like the hermit turned garbage into cake. When you understand that the cause of your suffering is none but you, the note stuck on your back, then problems begin to resolve. When you take responsibility for your faults, your inner mental predicaments and outer relationship problems vanish.

Whatever be your suffering, use it to attain the truth through contemplation. Understand the divine plan. If you witness God in you and others, start practicing forgiveness. Then suffering can turn into a means for attaining Self-realization. Whenever a karmic line manifests, seek forgiveness from God for yourself and for your ancestors. If you develop negative feelings for people, reprimand them or fight them while undergoing your suffering, then seek forgiveness from all of them through the spiritual practice of forgiveness. You can turnaround the cycle of suffering and karmic lines. Bondage itself will become a cause of freedom.

Seeker B: What is the way to cleanse karmic lines inherited through our genes so that they will not pass them to future generations?

Sirshree: Good thought! We think a lot about the next generation. We invest money for their future, we try to give them a good upbringing, we give them comforts and luxuries. But the most beneficial thing we can do for them is to cleanse our inherited karmic lines. When we do this, we not only benefit ourselves but also many future generations.

The spiritual practice of forgiveness has so much power that it can erase the karmic lines inherited from your ancestors and cleanse you inside out. The next generation will also be free from these lines. From now on, become aware of your physical, behavioral and mental karmic lines. Become vigilant to your beliefs and core thoughts. Erase karmic lines through the spiritual practice of forgiveness.

To do this, pray:

Dear GoD,
Please forgive me and my ancestors.
Please cleanse us from within.
I firmly believe that this is possible.
I have complete faith in you.
Please erase the karmic lines from my DNA.

Thank you for erasing all my karmic lines and restoring purity to my DNA.

Thank you. Thank you. Thank you.

Let Thy will be mine.

twenty

Seeker A: My aunt passed away few weeks ago. My family had no contact with her for several years because of a dispute over property matters. When I heard the news, all my childhood memories came to mind. I felt bad for not having visited her during her last days.

Since we didn't have the opportunity to reconcile with her, I was wondering whether I can seek forgiveness from her on behalf of everyone.

Sirshree: Yes, you can practice forgiveness here. This will help to cleanse the karmic lines with her.

Seeker A: But I don't believe I have any karmic lines with her. I haven't seen her since childhood.

Sirshree: That may be true. But at minimum, you can seek forgiveness for considering her to be a "separate body." Use everything as an opportunity to reinforce that neither you nor the people in your life are mere bodies. You all are manifestations of the same Consciousness that uses the body as a medium to express itself.

Seeker A: My family joined for her last rites. During the *Shradh* ceremony, the priests performed several prayers. I saw how these rites give us the opportunity to pay homage and tribute to the deceased. It would have been a good time to pray for her and seek forgiveness.

Sirshree: Over time, the true purpose of these rituals has been lost. You can pray and seek forgiveness now whether or not you did during the last rites. And speaking of last rites, it also helps to seek forgiveness on her behalf to everyone else – mentally. Seek forgiveness on behalf of your family members to her.

Seeker B: How would that help?

Sirshree: Suppose you haven't created any karmic lines, but your family members have? And she must have done so with them. When you seek forgiveness on their behalf for treating each other as "bodies", three things happen: You reinforce your true nature of the Universal Consciousness, your purity of mind is enhanced, and you help reduce the impact that karmic lines have created amongst your family members.

Seeker C: How often should I do this and who should I do it for?

Sirshree: At least once when someone dies. It helps to look at all the ancestors you know of, all those relatives that have passed on, and practice forgiveness once. You can seek forgiveness from them, seek forgiveness on their behalf, and seek forgiveness for the karmic lines passed down from them that are still affecting your present.

Seeker B: Your recommendation to mentally seek forgiveness for my ancestors' actions reminds me of the concept of morphic resonance that I recently read about. It is a process whereby self-organizing systems

---

* You can realize your true nature through direct experience by participating in the Magic of Awakening retreat, conducted by Tej Gyan Foundation. Read appendix for details.

inherit a memory from previous similar systems. Each individual inherits a collective memory from past members of the species. Each individual also contributes to the collective memory, affecting other members of the species in the future. Is this true?

Sirshree: Simply put, karmic lines cause injuries to the collective mind. You can imagine the collective mind as a universal field from where memories are borrowed and deposited back. From the beginning of human history, we have died from a variety of causes. Some died of severe wounds during battle; some died of illnesses. Some have been tortured; some have been abused or betrayed. All such incidents have caused injured memories, which impact the collective mind and in turn, the Universal Consciousness. Thus, in a way, they impact you, since all these injured memories impact the collective Consciousness.

Seeker A: Are you talking about reincarnation?

Sirshree: That's a topic for another day, especially once some of you have listened to the teachings on "Life After Death". For now, remember that every individual has some injured memories that are stored within them. How you lead your life determines how these memories are 'used' and shaped further.

If there is an injured memory of betrayal or backstabbing within you, you will be furious or insecure or depressed if someone betrays or deceives you. You'll feel as if you are going to die. For you, betrayal is equivalent to death because the ingrained past memories haven't healed yet. Others may wonder, "Why is he getting so angry over a petty issue?" They don't understand the memories that have been activated within you, and neither do you.

To make it even more simple, can you please share some fears you have or phobias you carry?

Seeker A: I am afraid of being alone at night. I am afraid of darkness.

Seeker C: I am afraid of heights. I feel like I'll fall to my death.

Sirshree: Yes, people have various kinds of phobias like fear of water, heights, accidents, air-travel, darkness, being alone, and many more. They are unaware of the cause of these phobias. Some people are so scared of fire that they even avoid lighting the gas stove. The point is that there are injured memories in each of us that cause these otherwise unexplainable fears. And forgiveness is one of the best ways to heal injured memories.

Fear can either arise from present life experiences or be inherited from the memory pool of the collective mind. There are many others before you who have collectively contributed to these fears. Historical incidents like the holocaust or acts of terrorism breed fear and leave deep scars on the collective mind.

Seeker B: But why are these injured memories carried forward in the first place?

Sirshree: When we consider ourselves to be a limited body-mind, such questions are but natural. If we look at everything from the perspective of the divine plan, we understand the mystery behind this. It is the Universal Self that expresses itself through all bodies. All the experiences are gathered by the Self and are available in the form of memories.

The Self re-uses memories in subsequent human bodies to bring about progressive evolution. You can see that every new generation is ahead of the previous one in terms of their level of understanding. This is why you find that children are cleverer than their predecessors. Inventions in each generation have paved the way for further inventions. This happens because the Self uses whatever experiences are gathered from a given generation to assist and improve the succeeding generations. Injured memories are also a part of the collective mind and are implanted in subsequent bodies in order to be healed, so that life can evolve and express its highest potential.

Seeker C: Thanks for this perspective shift. I now understand that our present lifetime offers opportunities for the Universal Self to heal injured memories and evolve. But how can we heal injured memories?

Sirshree: You are on the right track. The various situations in which injured memories surface are opportunities for healing. Those who have innate fears are supposed to overcome them by using these situations to heal these fears. Since this happens in the invisible realm, people fail to identify the opportunities disguised in the form of difficult situations. They become more restless and choose an impulsive fight-or-flight response. They either attack the other person or escape from the scene. But this doesn't heal their injured memories. Instead, new karmic lines are created, resulting in reinforcement of these injured memories.

Having understood the purpose behind injured memories, remind yourself, "This is an opportunity to heal my painful memories. I neither have to suppress them nor express them. They have emerged to get erased. I will face them by witnessing them in a detached manner when they arise as thoughts and feelings. I will not run away from this situation."

Contemplate about your injured memories that scare or upset you and heal them through the spiritual practice of forgiveness. Through this practice, you can heal the wounds in your subconscious mind with this understanding. Pray to GoD:

Dear GoD,

I seek forgiveness for the injured memories within me.

I seek forgiveness on behalf of all those
who have contributed to these injured memories.

Please forgive all of us and erase all the associated karmic lines that have been created in ignorance.

Thank you. Thank you. Thank you.

When you repeat this prayer several times a day, you will be freed from your past injured karmic lines. As soon as injured memories are healed, you will sense a noticeable change in your behavior. For example, you will no longer fear what you once did.

From now on, face all situations that nature is unfolding in your life with this understanding. Your mind may prompt you to run away and not face the unpleasant negative feelings and sensations in the body. At such times, reiterate this understanding:

This feeling has arisen to be healed.
Let this feeling be released from my body.
Let my mind become free from this feeling.
Thank you. Thank you. Thank you.

If you deal with every negative feeling in a detached manner and let go of it through the practice of forgiveness, then the intensity of your negative feelings will automatically reduce.

Seeker C: After learning about seeking forgiveness from the living and the dead, I was wondering about how to seek forgiveness from non-living objects. I heard that everything is energy vibrating at different frequencies. Even non-living things like televisions, computers, cars, houses, and chairs are all forms of the same universal energy. The experiments with water conducted by the scientist Dr. Emoto have concluded that our thoughts and emotions affect the inanimate things too. In Hinduism, some festivals are meant for paying respect and gratitude towards non-living objects. Should we practice forgiveness with objects too?

Sirshree: Yes, you may. Don't wait for any festival day for that. You can do it throughout the year. It will also raise your sensitivity. You can pray to them:

> *Please forgive me for not taking good care of you.*
> *I didn't see the Universal Consciousness in you.*
> *I considered you to be mere objects.*
> *I considered you separate from me and less significant than me.*
> *Please forgive me for my ignorance.*
> *Thank you for supporting me.*
> *Thank you. Thank you. Thank you.*

Some of you might find this funny. Remember, every time you practice forgiveness, it first cleanses your mind. If you find the practice of forgiveness on inanimate objects hard to digest, start with living beings first. Ensure you have practiced forgiveness with all your ancestors at least once. Practice forgiveness for your injured memories. Cleanse your karmic lines, injured memories and any hatred or guilt you are carrying. That is more important.

SECTION IV

Forgiveness for Ultimate Liberation

twenty-one

Seeker A: I am really happy that I'm not upset by daily life these days. My life is sailing smoothly. I feel compassion for everyone and pray for their wellbeing. I also perform good deeds. I have harmonious relationships with everyone. I'm really contented and can't think of a better state than this.

Sirshree: It's a very good state to be in. This is a state where you have moved from negativity to virtuousness. You have got rid of the snakes of sorrow and only ladders of joy remain. You want to stay in this happy and contented state. But this poses the biggest obstacle in your journey towards complete liberation.

Seeker B: How can that be?

Sirshree: This state is like a plateau and is the toughest to cross. If you consider it the final goal and rest here, there is a probability of backsliding into your old state. It is common for the human mind to become complacent, egoistic and arrogant. You can feel superior to others. When this happens, the ladder that was a means for progress becomes a trap. It becomes a permanent home and you forget to proceed to your real home, which lies beyond snakes and ladders.

Virtuousness is not good when it entraps you. It's like being bound with golden handcuffs. They might be golden, but they are handcuffs after all. Iron handcuffs, borne out of sorrow, are painful, but golden handcuffs give a sense of pleasure. We feel aversion for the iron handcuffs and attachment to the golden ones. If only we knew that they halt our journey to liberation.

Your real goal is to go beyond virtuousness. You have moved from bad to good but now you have to go even further because beyond good is where God exists. The good that traps you is not good. The good that prevents you from reaching God is as bad as bad. If you get stuck here, the purpose for which you are born on Earth – to experientially know who you truly are – remains unfulfilled.

Seeker C: I am hearing you say that we should progress even beyond. How do we continue to progress?

Sirshree: Making progress by moving ahead from a plateau requires true devotion. Devotion has the power to detach you from the biggest distractions. When the ego doesn't allow you to surrender, devotion comes to your rescue. It helps you surrender the strongest tendencies, beliefs and core thoughts. No matter how difficult it is to forgive, devotion makes it easy for you. Devotion doesn't mean mere chanting or rituals. When devotion comes into action, even the impossible becomes possible.

In true devotion, you surrender yourself to the will of God and can easily say "Your will is my will." You submit to God's divine plan and allow Him to experience and express His divine qualities through your body-mind. You free yourself from the entanglements, which create the notion of being a separate individual. You begin to treat everything with an attitude of evenness.

This state is beyond like and dislike, aversion and craving, pain and pleasure, praise and blame, success and failure, or fame and shame. Till now, we have discussed about practicing forgiveness to dissolve the snakes in your life. But now, we are discussing a higher dimension of the practice, which leads you beyond both snakes and ladders. The practice of forgiveness helps you transcend both snakes and ladders and attain the blissful state of liberation.

Seeker A: I have always considered devotion as an unnecessary aspect since I've believed it to be the mere ritual of chanting and singing of hymns. I feel that my devotion is not strong enough to move beyond the state of 'goodness' to complete liberation. What can I do?

Sirshree: Pray to GoD to strengthen your devotion:

Dear GoD,

Please forgive me for my tendencies, distractions, karmic lines and anything else that is obstructing my devotion.

Please cleanse me from within.

Please help me to go beyond both goodness and negativity.

Please empower my devotion and augment it.

Thank you. Thank you. Thank you.

twenty-two

Seeker B: Can you please explain more about the state of complete liberation?

Sirshree: Before that, it's important to understand the real cause of karmic bondage. The body, by itself, is inert and can't produce karmic lines. Self or Consciousness is the enlivening principle, which is beyond karmic lines. But when the Self forgets its true nature, it identifies itself with the limited body-mind. In the process, the Universal 'I' assumes itself as a separate individual 'I'. We call this ego.

This false 'I' is strengthened whenever you are hurt or appreciated. As long as the ego exists, karmic lines are formed and you remain entangled in the game of snakes and ladders. But when you understand that the individual 'I' is an illusion and realize your true nature, you transcend the game and abide as the whiteboard of the Universal Self.*

You realize that you, the Universal 'I', are enlivening this game. You can remain entangled in the game for as long as you want or choose liberation. Once you are liberated from karmic bondage, all deeds are performed through the body spontaneously. No one remains to say, "I did it." You transcend the three qualities of the body-mind – inertia (*tamas*), action or dynamism (*rajas*), and balance (*satva*). Instead of becoming their slave, you use them to experience and express divine qualities. You may use the quality of inertia during meditation, the quality of action or dynamism while engaging in your daily tasks, and the quality of balance for rendering selfless service.

When you operate from your true nature, you realize that Self is playing this game of snakes and ladders with Himself through different body-minds to experience love and joy. When you remember this truth, you live life playfully. You allow everything to happen spontaneously. You watch life unfold with a feeling of detached passion.

When you forget this truth, you take the game seriously and make everything that happens a matter of life and death. You rejoice in your successes and mourn your defeats. Having received this understanding, you can progress spiritually.

Let's further understand this with an example.

In the Indian epic Mahabharata, as long as Arjuna was assuming himself as a separate individual in the battlefield, he was experiencing the agony of killing his near and dear ones. But when Lord Krishna made him aware of his true nature, he was liberated from his attachments, dilemma and sorrow. He became free from the illusion of being a separate individual. In place of the feeling that "I have to perform", he received the understanding that "Self is enacting through my body, I am merely a medium to enact the will of the Self." From this standpoint of detached witnessing, when he fought in the battlefield and killed many warriors, as per the story of the Mahabharata, none of his karma created karmic lines since he remained a non-doer of his karma. In place of an "individual" Arjuna, the Self was functioning through his body.

Seeker C: I'd like to be free from ego. I'd like to live by being who I truly am.

Sirshree: Practice forgiveness to be liberated from the false 'I'. Whenever you think "I did this", immediately seek forgiveness from GoD:

Dear GoD,

All that is happening through the medium of this body is actually owing to your presence.

Please forgive this body-mind for assuming itself to be the doer in ignorance and unconsciousness.

Please erase all its lines of individualism.

Please wipe away its sense of separateness.

Please cleanse it from within.

Please empty it of all its negativities and prepare it for Your divine expression.

Let it become a medium for the expression of who You truly are, not the ego.

Let Your will be this body's will.

Thank you. Thank you. Thank you.

In this world, everyone is trying to become something else. Everyone wants to get promoted at work, become a parent, or a grandparent, a leader, or an engineer. As soon as you become something, you forget who you truly are. You tend to forget that you are the all-pervading omnipotent, Universal Self. You cannot be made bigger or smaller. Self is as it has always been; it has not become anything. All "becoming" is merely a game of beliefs.

Whenever your ego tries to belittle the Self by feeling superior to others, tell yourself: "*You have always been complete. You cannot be made bigger or smaller.*" Seek forgiveness from GoD for this feeling:

Dear GoD,

Please forgive me for forgetting my true nature.

Please forgive me for getting into the crazy game of trying to become something superior.

Please forgive me for my ignorance and unconsciousness.

Thank you. Thank you. Thank you.

Seeker A: This is beautiful Sirshee. Now, I will progress spiritually.

Sirshree: It is all grace. Let the mind become pure and transparent so that the Self shines. Let there not be any sense of doer-ship in progressing spiritually. Forgiveness helps in adding humility and remembering who is behind it all. Open yourself to the flow of grace.

twenty-three

Seeker B: I would like to make progress in today's competitive world. I want to be well known in my profession, I wish to be wealthy and financially independent. But is it wrong to pursue my individualistic goals in the light of what we are learning? If I want to grow spiritually, should I give up my existing profession and render only altruistic service?

Sirshree: Many people often have such questions. Is it wrong to acquire fame or wealth? They wonder whether material success can ever go hand-in-hand with spiritual growth.

There is nothing inherently wrong with any kind of deed you perform. The intention behind your deed decides whether it is personal or altruistic. If your thoughts are centered on words like I, me, mine, then those deeds are personal and lead to the fulfilment of your personal goals.

For example, as part of a personal goal, a student thinks, "I should apply to a reputed engineering college. Then I will be successful." An engineer thinks, "I should get a good job and settle down, then I'll be successful." An employee thinks, "I should climb the corporate ladder to seek a top position, earn better salary and buy every luxury. Then I'll be successful."

Everyone ceaselessly strives hard to achieve their personal goals, only to find the next goal in the pipeline. The deeds being the same, if the intention behind them is changed, they become altruistic.

With this changed perspective, the student may think, "I should apply to a reputed engineering college so that I can gain core engineering skills and learn the latest technology." The engineer may think, "I should get a good job to contribute my skills for the advancement of all at the global level." The employee may think, "I should be able to improve my performance so that I can deliver services that solve a problem for our customers."

When you render altruistic service, you not only benefit yourself, but also others.

Here is one more example:

There are two movie producers. The first makes an action movie with the intention to attract as many viewers as possible and earn a lot of profit. The second producer makes a movie that depicts higher values of life with the intention to spread love, joy and peace to as many viewers as possible. He would like them to imbibe these principles and lead a life of Higher Consciousness. Both producers are doing the same job. But the first one's goal is personal and second one's goal is impersonal or altruistic. It's not that the second producer benefits only others and not himself. He benefits both himself and others. Most importantly, he is contributing to the divine expression of Self.

You can enjoy a perfect life with harmony in relationships, financial freedom and physical vitality even while rendering altruistic service or living life impersonally as opposed to living a personal life. Karmic lines arise due to the intention behind your deed, not due to the deed itself. If you perform all deeds selflessly, remain detached from their fruits, and remember who is performing the deeds and why, then you will not create karmic lines.

A single universal power is providing thoughts to each body and getting deeds done through them to take life forward. Every life form is contributing towards this supreme power, be it creation or destruction. Though you attach a negative connotation to destruction, creation and destruction are two sides of the same coin. Destruction is an essential aspect of creation. It paves the way for creation. If you understand this, you will come out of your limited viewpoint and surrender to the will of God.

Seeker A: How can my deeds as a housewife become altruistic?

Sirshree: Humans cannot live one moment without action. We constantly perform deeds either through our bodies or through our thoughts. Even if you decided not to act, you would be performing the deed of inaction. When you perform deeds with a selfless intention, for the wellbeing of others, then you render altruistic service regardless of wherever you are—at home, at the workplace, or in the market. Always understand that karmic lines arise out of the intention behind your deed, and not out of the deed itself. You may engage in an altruistic service but due to lack of understanding, it may turn out to be an individual selfish deed resulting in the formation of karmic lines. On the other hand, if you perform an individual deed with a proper understanding, it can become an altruistic service.

Let's understand it with an example:

A rich man makes a substantial donation to the poor with the intention of earning fame. Although his deed may seem altruistic, his selfish intention makes it personal and creates karmic lines.

On the other hand, a cook works in a restaurant. While cooking, he has noble intentions. He thanks God for the opportunity to feed people. He wants his food to give people joy and health. His pure feelings turn his regular job into an altruistic service.

You don't have to do anything extra to render altruistic service. With proper understanding, each of your deeds, including homemaking, can become altruistic and you can lead a selfless life, free of karmic bondages.

Seeker C: That's a great insight! But usually people think that you endure a lot of hardship in a selfless life. You work for others and don't get anything in return. They think that it is only others who reap the benefits of the work you have done.

Sirshree: This is not true. In fact, there can be none happier than the one who leads a selfless life and understands its true meaning. A selfless impersonal life actually benefits you more than it benefits others.

When you pursue individual desires or goals, you get attached to them. Sometimes, in an attempt to fulfil them, you may get into transgressions that can pollute your thoughts and deeds. You compare yourself with others and this gives rise to vices like jealousy, hatred and resentment. If you attain your desire, it boosts your ego and in turn it gives birth to many more desires. You become greedier. If your desires aren't fulfilled, you become a victim of sadness, depression and yearning.

In short, selfish desires give rise to vices and bloat the ego. On the other hand, if your desires are selfless, you are safeguarded from these perils. You perform all deeds passionately, but without getting attached to their outcome. Leading a selfless life is devotion in itself. It protects you from all the evils of the world and makes you pure and pious. The more selfless service you render, the purer you become.

The world is an expression of the Self. The Self is manifesting through everyone. We need to think how we can best contribute to His Self-expression. God has gifted everyone with something special. Some can cook well, some can sing well, some can organize and manage activities well, some can write well, some can read well, and so forth. Everyone has special qualities. We need to hone these qualities and use them to contribute selflessly to God's Self-expression. Many great souls like Lord Buddha, Saint Gyaneshwar, Saint Kabir, Mahatma Gandhi, and Mother Teresa, have spent their lives for the welfare of others.

Seeker C: But all these great souls were born on Earth for a selfless purpose. They received a specific upbringing and training from childhood. They were free from family responsibilities. How can ordinary people like us lead selfless lives even if we wish to? If we utilize our skills for rendering selfless service, how can we earn our livelihood? How can we look after our families? How can we lead selfless lives with all these responsibilities?

Sirshree: You can still lead a selfless life even while fulfilling your individual responsibilities and taking care of your development. Just keep a selfless intention while performing all your deeds. Without changing your goal and deeds, just change the intention and outlook behind them and they will become selfless. Your purpose in life will become altruistic. You can continue to earn your livelihood and take care of your family, but your intention behind all this can be selfless.

A visionary has said, "It is one of life's beautiful laws that whenever someone truly helps somebody, it is impossible not to receive help for himself." Those who cure others, heal themselves. Those who donate a part of their wealth receive immeasurable wealth from nature. Those who try to raise others' level of consciousness themselves rise to great levels of consciousness. With a big heart, start leading a selfless life. You too will benefit along with others. And above all you will stay away from creating new karmic lines.

twenty-four

Seeker B: If keeping an altruistic intention behind our deeds can free us from creating karmic lines, why doesn't everyone have this understanding?

Sirshree: It's not just the intention; you also need the complete knowledge of the principle of karma and bondage. When you put the understanding into practice, you become free from karmic lines. The real question is: how can people gain this understanding which can liberate them from karmic bondages? What do you think?

Seeker B: Yes, that's true. Many try to find answers on the Internet.

Seeker A: Some people refer to spiritual scriptures like the Vedas, Puranas, and Upanishads for this understanding.

Seeker C: Some refer to holy books like the Quran, Bible, or Guru Granth Sahib to find this profound wisdom. There are some who also get this knowledge from hearsay.

Sirshree: All of you are right. However, the knowledge that is being distributed in the name of spirituality has become adulterated. By using such concocted interpretations, people either stray away from the path or get stuck at the wrong places.

Seeker C: Why does this happen?

Sirshree: To understand this, we need to see how it all began. Man's spiritual quest is ancient. For thousands of years, he has been seeking answers to questions like "Who am I? Who is God? Who created this world and why? What are the laws that govern the universe? What is the purpose of my existence in this world? What is karma? What is destiny?"

Some saints and yogis received answers to these questions through experience, by following the path of meditation, yoga, and devotion. They even documented these answers for the benefit of posterity in the form of holy scriptures like the Vedas, Puranas, Upanishads, Quran, Bible, Guru Granth Sahib, and many more.

However, the knowledge given in these ancient religious scriptures was suited to the needs of those times. People of those times had a different language, a different set of needs, different social ethos. In today's context, when the same scriptures are read, their interpretations can vary based on the reader's level of consciousness and understanding. As a result, the true meaning of these scriptures is lost. People have even twisted the scriptures to suit their own propaganda and convenience. By propagating such corrupt interpretations of the knowledge to the masses, they have harmed themselves and also in turn, the society. They have created karmic lines not only for themselves, but also for the generations to come.

Seeker C: I understand that they harmed themselves by creating karmic lines. But how does it cause harm to future generations?

Sirshree: Let's understand this with an example:

When a child doesn't get attention, he throws tantrums. The parents then pacify him by showering love and attention upon him. The child considers this is a good ploy to get attention. He doesn't realize that he is creating bondage for himself. At that time, he can only see temporary benefits. He can only see the attention that he is getting.

In the same way, people have been troubled with the whims of their mind and are overpowered by mental tantrums. At such times, they seek solace in spiritual knowledge. They are interested in quick relief so they twist and turn this knowledge to suit their immediate needs. This temporarily solves their problems. They tweak the knowledge of the scriptures to gratify their egos and the knowledge that they pass to future generations is one that appeases the mind instead of transcending it. True knowledge serves to transcend the ego; it serves to go beyond the dramas that the mind plays.

In the future, when people seek support from such 'tweaked' knowledge, they won't receive the desired result. They'll be misguided and in turn they'll lose faith. They will be deprived of attaining their supreme goal in life and remain entangled in the emotional dramas and tendencies of their mind. Those who twist this knowledge not only harm themselves, but their karmic lines pose big hurdles for future generations.

Seeker B: So, what's the way out for someone who is earnest in his seeking of the truth?

Sirshree: Here, the guru's role is pivotal. A true guru simplifies what appears to be complex and conveys only the essential wisdom which is required for your liberation.

Here is one more example to understand this:

People used to ask Lord Buddha a lot of questions on spirituality. "Where does the soul go after the body's death? What is heaven like? What does God look like?" Buddha would remain silent when asked such questions. Upon further prodding, he would repeat only one sentence, "The One who is beyond has kept this unexpressed."

Once, to explain things to his disciples, Buddha picked up some leaves lying on the ground and said, "There are many more leaves on the tree than those in my hand. I have given you only as much wisdom as there is in my hand. There is much more wisdom, but it is not essential for your liberation. Implement the principles that I have taught you and be free from sorrow. Don't indulge in matters that please your intellect. All you need to do is make good use of your time, have right mindfulness, right concentration and right wisdom. With these, you shall attain nirvana."

Instead of dwelling in the 'what' and 'why' of knowledge, which the intellect delights in, the guru deals with the 'how'. This is where the mind is made to surrender to the truth. The guru bids the seeker to follow those minimal instructions which will help the seeker make progress. By following this action plan, the seeker is safeguarded from karmic lines and steadily progresses toward the supreme truth.

twenty-five

Seeker A: Can you please tell us some essential teachings, which can help us progress? Can you please give us a plan that will protect us from karmic lines and help us attain the supreme truth?

Sirshree: Can you specify the points on which you need guidance?

Seeker A: While I am a proud woman, I've always felt that I should have been born a boy. Boys can afford to relax at home, whereas girls have to balance between the workplace and homemaking. Also, I've always felt that my parents could have been more supportive to me like my friend's parents were to her.

Sirshree: It is common for people to have regrets over their birth. They hold onto the "could've" and "should've" of the past and draw karmic lines in the process. This not only affects their present negatively, but also plants seeds for repeated occurrences in their future.

Accept what you received at birth. You cannot change your body; whether it's male or female. Neither can you change the family you were born into, nor your family members. Accept your family and your body as they are. Non-acceptance increases the mind's chatter, which creates karmic lines. Seek forgiveness for these karmic lines.

Seeker A: Right. I didn't realize that I have been creating karmic lines by resisting my family and myself. I need to accept my family and myself wholeheartedly.

Sirshree: Good. What do others have to share?

Seeker C: When I see mouth-watering dishes. I just can't resist and I tend to overeat. What should I do to overcome this strong tendency?

Sirshree: You can overcome your strong tendencies with even stronger deeds. If you wish to eliminate strong tendencies, then perform actions that have strong intent and resolve. In this case, when you are in front of your favorite dish, pause and observe what the exact feeling is. Ask what you would lose if you controlled your intake? Does indulgence in food help you achieve your ultimate goal? When you are reminded of this goal, it becomes possible to keep away from these tendencies. For each tendency you want to get rid of, you will have to perform the strong action of raising your level of understanding and seeking forgiveness for harboring the tendency. You can then break free and transform them to align with the light of higher wisdom.

While you are doing this work, you can't ignore your subtle tendencies. You may consider them to be negligible and think that they will not cause you harm. But even a small tendency can put your liberation at stake. Persistently observe, identify and remove every subtle tendency.

You may need to take this quite seriously. When you notice recurring incidents in your life, contemplate and reflect on their cause. Why does this keep happening? When things happen repeatedly, consider that you could yourself be responsible for it. Closely monitor your behavior. Contemplate and write these incidents down, along with your insights. Through constant observation, contemplation and evaluation, you will recognize your subtler tendencies. Once you bring them to light, it is easy to break them.

Seeker C: Can prayer help in this regard?

Sirshree: Yes, you can pray to safeguard yourself from all tendencies. When you pray, you connect to the Self. Prayer has the power to attract grace. When you fail to understand why certain things are happening in your life, relentlessly offer prayers. When emotions like fear, greed or lust overpower you, keep praying until the tendency loosens its grip.

Since ancient times, people have been taught to chant mantras to annihilate the effect of their tendencies. Praying and chanting are meant to raise your level of awareness. They remind you to endure the consequences of karmic lines gracefully and allow a fresh response with love and devotion.

Seeker B: When I perform good deeds I feel like telling everyone. But I shy away from disclosing my sins.

Sirshree: Don't conceal your sins and don't flaunt your good deeds. This way, the effect of the fruits of your deeds diminishes. Further, they loosen their grip on you. Even after rendering selfless service, those who seek credit and praise for their virtuous deeds miss the ultimate goal of Self-realization. Don't hanker after recognition or publicity for your good deeds. And if you have sinful thoughts or you sin, admit it honestly to yourself, your guru, a spiritual guide or your true friend. When you reveal your bad deeds, the consequences of those deeds and their corresponding karmic bondage reduce. For this reason, it is advised not to conceal anything from your guru.

Mahatma Gandhi revealed the wrong deeds performed during his childhood in his autobiography. His true repentance shines through the pages and no wonder he emerged as a great soul. If you take a cue from his life and learn to disclose your bad deeds, you are taking a major step towards freedom.

At the very least, don't hide anything from yourself. Don't deceive yourself by making excuses. Disclose your sins to your guru or a spiritual guide either verbally or in writing in order to be free from them. Jesus taught people how to repent in the right way. If you confess your sins in detail, you are more inclined to move forward; superficial repentance won't bring change. Repentance is important because it reduces the ill effects of sin and prevents you from repeating them.

Seeker C: I decided to not get angry. Sometimes I succeed, sometimes I fail.

Sirshree: You need to raise your sensitivity. The time between stimulus and response is infinitesimal. Reactions are programmed responses to external and internal stimuli. Become alert in this gap to choose a right response. Once you react to a stimulus, you can't change your response. You need to raise your sensitivity and level of awareness in this time gap. It is the doorway to freedom from bondage.

When you shift your awareness to the space between stimulus and response, your actions no longer create karmic lines. If your actions are driven by karmic lines, they will create more karmic lines in the future. Before taking action, ask yourself, "Am I doing this with my own understanding or as a compulsive reaction to someone's behavior?"

Let's understand it with an example:

If someone swears at you and you retaliate, you are bound by karmic lines. If you respond with awareness by seeing Consciousness in the other, you are acting with awareness.. You are not being a victim of your programmed responses. There is conscious choice, instead of compulsion.

Let your understanding guide you. Let it become a torch on your path. Never react based on how people behaved with you. Their behavior may change, but don't let your torch of understanding flicker.

Seeker A: I feel that I have limited my life to homemaking and regret not having taken up a salaried job. How should I motivate myself to lead a selfless life?

Sirshree: Always understand that all personalized deeds create karmic lines. When you perform selfless deeds for the wellbeing of others, karmic lines are not created. You remain free.

You can be motivated by the examples of the great masters like Lord Buddha or Jesus Christ. How much salary would you pay them for their service to humanity? They rendered the highest service relentlessly. But they didn't need money because their lives were completely selfless. Their deeds created no karmic lines.

Start with wherever you are now. See how you can contribute to the all-round growth of your family by expanding your care to touch their lives spiritually. You can then consider expanding the span of your selfless presence beyond the family.

Seeker B: Please guide us on how to perform karma without attachment?

Sirshree: When you perform karma that is free of reaction and attachment, you won't create karmic bondage. It's like a line drawn in the sky. When a line is carved in stone, it remains forever. When a line is drawn on sand, it remains until it is blown away by the wind. When a line is drawn in water, it dissolves immediately. Beyond all this is a line drawn in the sky, for such a line is not even a line. It doesn't create any future karma. Your karma becomes the expression of the Self; free from the individual ego and, opening the doorway to liberation.

You can also renounce your karma. Here, renunciation doesn't imply renunciation of deeds, but rather the renunciation of doer-ship. Karma will happen but the myth that "I am doing this" will vanish. In this state, you are free from the belief that you are the body.

As you practice abiding in Consciousness through meditation and go beyond doer-ship, the state of liberation will assert itself from within and you will feel free from all bondage. Your reference point will shift and you will begin to view everything from the standpoint of the Self. No habit or tendency can attach you to your body. Your body becomes a medium for the expression of divine qualities like unconditional love, compassion, courage, peace and creativity.

Seeker C: When I help someone and they don't reciprocate, I feel angry. What can I do about this feeling?

Sirshree: Deal with the Source, not the channel. In reality, all our dealings should only be with the one Source – God, Self, Universal Consciousness – which enlivens everything.

When man receives anything, he assumes the channel through which he receives – to be the Source. As a result, he expects to receive further from the same channel and becomes disheartened if the channel does not deliver the goods. For example, if his brother, who used to help him earlier, stops helping him, he laments that his brother has let him down. This is so because people assume their relatives to be the givers, the Source.

We ignorantly court sorrow when we get habituated to desire from the channels around us. When we need water, we draw it from the tap. Does the tap have any capacity of giving? The tap is merely a channel for the water reservoir. There are many taps through which water is received, but they all come from the same water reservoir in the building. When we insist that we want water only from a particular tap, we invite sorrow in our lives.

If you seek water directly from the reservoir, you will get more than you could ever ask for. You give up your limited perspective of expecting from a particular channel. As a result, you realize that there are many other channels through which the Self can give.

Stop dealing with individuals and begin to see the Self in them. You give to the Self and receive from the Self through all your dealings in the world. You will not expect anything from individuals as you rest in faith that everything that has to come, will come from the Self. This way, you won't create karmic lines and move towards liberation.

Seek forgiveness for dealing with individuals and expecting from the channels instead of the Source.

twenty-six

Seeker A: I see many people practice chanting, rituals or penance in the name of liberation, yet I see them struggling for worldly achievements. Why is this so?

Sirshree: As discussed previously, the intent behind every karma decides its outcome. Although they may be practicing these techniques in the name of liberation, their hidden intent could be to fulfil their personal desires, like attaining worldly success, health, or occult powers. Even if they manage to free themselves from the iron handcuffs of sorrow, they become bound by the golden handcuffs of pleasure. This isn't true freedom from karmic bondage.

Seeker B: What is it that liberates us from karmic bondage in a true sense?

Sirshree: Liberation results from selfless devotion which is devoid of any personal desires. Devotion shouldn't have any traces of the individual 'I' or the ego. Otherwise, one may remain immersed in devotion for a long time but not be free from karmic bondage because of one's ego, which takes credit also for the act of devotion. In true devotion the devotee completely surrenders his ego. Rendering selfless service is also a kind of devotion. It is called 'devotion-in-action'. The first step is to give up the false 'I'.

Seeker C: But it's our habit to say 'I'. Everything in life revolves around this 'I'. Is it possible to get rid of it?

Sirshree: If it's possible with one, it's possible with everyone. You are habituated to saying 'I' because you have seen people around you doing the same since you were born. But with the wisdom you have received, and your raised level of awareness, you can experiment with techniques to break this habit.

Seeker C: Can you suggest a technique?

Sirshree: Count the number of times you think or say 'I' during the day. This will raise your awareness.

Seeker A: It seems very simple to practice. But of what use is it?

Sirshree: With practice, you'll become more aware of using the word 'I' in your speech and thoughts and will avoid using it. You'll begin to say things differently. For example, instead of saying "I saw it," you will say, "It was seen." Instead of saying "I did it," you will say, "It was done." Instead of saying "I think this," you will say, "A thought occurred."

You'll become aware and alert about your thoughts and speech. You will be constantly reminded that you aren't the individual 'I', but the Universal Self – a witness to all happenings. All that is happening through the medium of your body is owing to the presence of the Self. Gradually, this truth will be instilled in the depths of your mind. It will happen automatically, without conscious effort. You'll become a detached witness and a non-doer of the deeds happening through the medium of your body. The deeds will not bind you in karmic bondage and you'll gain complete freedom! Before you go to sleep at night, seek forgiveness for all the events where you assumed yourself to be a separate 'I'.

Seeker C: Sometimes, in day-to-day situations, it's difficult to avoid using the word 'I'. What should we do at times like this?

Sirshree: You may use the word 'I' in those situations. But be clear from within who this 'I' is that you are referring to. Always remember that 'I' is the Universal Self.

In the Indian epic, the Ramayana, during the war, the demon Ravana's ten heads were chopped off several times, but he was not killed. The heads would reappear. But one arrow that was shot at his navel was enough to kill him.

Consider your false 'I' as the navel of the demon Ravana. If you eliminate your false 'I' and let the Universal Self operate in its place, the web of your karmic lines will collapse. Then the Self alone will express itself through your body. You become established in this state, leading to liberation during embodiment in this very lifetime.

Seeker B: Sometimes, after performing a deed, even when I say that "This deed was done through my body" my mind arises and chatters, "This is good. This is bad. This shouldn't have been done this way. This is right and that is wrong."

Sirshree: What is more important – the deeds that you perform or your thoughts during and after you perform the deeds? When you have the right understanding, you will say that deeds are no doubt important, but the viewpoint with which you look at the deeds is more important. Things happen that require action, and this isn't always in your control. Focus on the running commentary of your mind during or after the action.

The mind constantly chatters during and after incidents and deeds. If you think, "*I* did this," a karmic line of ego is created. To avoid fuelling your ego and shifting away from your true Self, always say, "It happened through me; through the medium of my body."

Check your feelings behind every action you perform. Avoid the feeling of doer-ship by surrendering all deeds to God. Be a detached witness. If you are exercising, observe your body doing the exercises. *You are with your body, but you are not the body. The body is only a companion.* Remind yourself, "My companion is working out, not me."

Seeker A: It's fine to surrender deeds to God. But when the fruit of the action is satisfactory, we get attached to it.

Sirshree: When you receive the fruit of your actions, surrender it to God. If you perform your deeds with the feeling of doer-ship there can be only three possible results: sorrow, joy or confusion. Seek forgiveness and surrender them to God by saying, "O God, this joy is yours, this sorrow is yours, this confusion is also yours. Please forgive me."

Whenever an incident happens, check the feelings within. If you feel happy, instead of thinking "I felt happy," surrender the happiness to God by saying, "This happiness is yours." If you surrender only sorrow and not joy, you will again receive sorrow. If you are confused or suffering, surrender both to God. When you surrender every fruit of action to God, you won't be attached to the fruit, neither will you be obsessed by it. It won't become a cause of bondage for you. Instead, it will bring you completeness leading to your liberation.

Seeker B: Agreed, we can surrender the sorrow and confusion to God. But how can we endure the suffering we go through in the process?

Sirshree: When you are completely immersed in the love and devotion of God, the suffering becomes a parcel from God. You gracefully endure it without complaint or worry. This is the hallmark of a true devotee.

The lives of devotees like saint Meera and Jesus have been living demonstrations of how we should endure parcels. True devotion allowed Jesus to submit himself to the divine order at the time of crucifixion. He suffered torture, but sought only forgiveness from God for his perpetrators. Immersed in devotion, saint Meera didn't complain when she was forced to drink poison. She didn't grumble about the pain. Instead she happily submitted herself to the divine will. Socrates and Mansoor were so engrossed in devotion and their spiritual practice that they never gave a thought to the suffering their body had to endure. True devotion made it possible for Lord Buddha and Lord Mahavir to renounce their material comforts and endure the rigors of a life of recluse in search of the ultimate truth of life.

In love and devotion, we don't notice suffering because we revel in the bliss of devotion itself without the need of any favorable result. This is the grandeur of devotion. It makes us so powerful and steadfast within, that sorrow doesn't seem like sorrow. When devotion rises in your life, you will rise above all karma. Rising to the heights of devotion should be the ultimate goal of life. Seeking forgiveness helps in this. Forgiveness is the beginning and devotion is the end. It leads to the heights of devotion.

twenty-seven

Seeker C: We have learned various prayers for forgiveness in a variety of contexts, all pertaining to different karmic lines. Is there a single consolidated practice that we can follow regularly that will touch all the aspects of karmic lines and cleanse us fully from within?

Sirshree: It is essential that you invest your time and attention in cleansing each facet of your life so that you purify yourself from within deeply and fully. However, if you want to address all the facets of purification through a single process, you can practice Complete Forgiveness meditation.

This meditation technique addresses all karmic lines to free you all at once. If you practice this meditation before bed every night, you will begin to experience purity, lightness and freedom. All the positive things that are yet to come into your life, like physical vitality, peace of mind, harmony in relationships, wisdom, abundance of love, joy, wealth, and success, will then reach you smoothly.

You may set a timer for a particular duration and practice this meditation. Follow the steps carefully:

1. Sit in a comfortable meditative posture and close your eyes.
2. Reinforce your intention by telling yourself, "I am about

to practice forgiveness meditation. It is going to benefit me immensely. All my karmic lines will be erased."

3. Now remind yourself: I am practicing forgiveness because I negatively contributed to the creation of karmic lines out of ignorance. I have strengthened these lines through my thoughts and feelings. Whatever wrongs I see, hear or experience, the vices I see are a result of my contribution to them. I am responsible for removing my negative contributions through the practice of forgiveness so that I can shift from the individual 'I' to the Universal Self.

4. Invite the God of Dusting into your field of awareness. With God (or guru or any source of inspiration) as your witness, repeat this prayer a few times:

Dear GoD,
Please help me to forgive myself.
Please help me to cleanse myself within.
Please help me to love myself.
Please help me to accept myself.
Please purify my inner being.

5. Feel as if this is happening. GoD is listening to your prayer and also answering. You have sought forgiveness for everything that you have done so far. GoD forgives you for this. Also forgive yourself. Love yourself like you love a child. Tell yourself from the bottom of your heart:

I have forgiven you.
I accept the way you are.
I respect you. I always love you.

6. Forgive yourself for all the karmic lines you have knowingly or unknowingly formed. For example, you may have unknowingly caused trouble to someone. Tell yourself, "I forgive you for all such incidents." Let all lines be erased. Recall all the incidents and people in order – A to Z – to the extent possible. Forgive yourself for every incident that has happened with them. Only when you forgive yourself can you seek forgiveness from others and forgive them. This first step is essential for increasing your inner strength.

7. With an open heart tell yourself, "Let go... Let go..." Don't hold onto any line. Let go of lines held deeply within your mind. Tell yourself:

> *All that happened based on the situation*
> *and my level of understanding at that time.*
> *It's now the past. Let go of the guilt.*
> *Let it go. I forgive you.*

Remind yourself:

> *GoD is cleansing me from within.*
> *He is helping me forgive myself.*
> *The power of God, nature and guru can easily erase*
> *the thickest of my karmic lines.*
> *All my lines are being erased right now.*
> *Guilt and sadness are being released.*

8. Sit in a posture that evokes devotion. You may fold your hands and join them, raise your hands, or open your arms. Sitting in this posture, tell yourself:

I cleanse myself of every guilt and sadness.
I forgive myself one hundred percent.

9. Seek forgiveness from everyone you've knowingly or unknowingly hurt. Tell them in your mind:

Please forgive me for hurting you
knowingly or unknowingly through my words or actions.
Please forgive me for not seeing
the Universal Consciousness in you.
I am sorry. I will try my best not to repeat this.
Thank you for forgiving me.
Thank you. Thank you. Thank you.

10. Seek forgiveness wholeheartedly on behalf of the entire world and remove your negative contribution.

No one else is at fault for the problems that I am seeing in the world.
I am at fault because it is happening in my field of awareness.
Please forgive me for my ignorance and semi-unconsciousness.
Please forgive me for my negative contribution to the problems.

11. If you feel some people are not worthy of forgiveness, don't forgive them but cleanse them. Pray for them:

Dear GoD,

Please cleanse them from within.

Please eradicate their sinful tendencies.

Let these people too receive wisdom.

Let their understanding and consciousness rise.

*Please bestow upon them the same grace
that you have bestowed upon me.*

Please make them worthy to receive your grace.

*Please forgive me as I saw them as culprits
and failed to see your divine presence in them.*

12. Seek forgiveness for the lines you drew with non-living objects. Speak to them:

    Please forgive me for not taking good care of you.

    I didn't see the Universal Consciousness in you.

    I considered you to be mere objects.

    I considered you separate from me and less significant than me.

    Thank you for supporting me at all times.

13. Seek forgiveness for the lines associated with your health. Seek forgiveness for the negative thoughts you have held about your body parts, like, "My height is not good enough, my weight is not proper, I don't have a good complexion, my hair is unhealthy," and so on. By seeking an apology with love and acceptance, your body will become healthy and strong. Pray to ailing body parts:

I failed to pay attention to you all these years.

Please forgive me for my carelessness and ignorance.

I love you. From now on, I will take care of you.

I will never do anything that causes you trouble.

I am grateful to you for your unconditional love and support.

Thank you. Thank you. Thank you.

14. Seek forgiveness for your ego, the false 'I'.

Dear GoD,

All that is happening through the medium of this body is actually owing to Your presence.

Please forgive this body for assuming itself to be a doer, in ignorance and unconsciousness.

Please erase all its lines of individualism.

Please wipe away its sense of separateness.

Please cleanse it from within.

Please empty it of all its negativities and prepare it for Your expression.

Let it become a medium for Your divine expression, not the ego.

Let Your will be this body's will.

Thank you. Thank you. Thank you.

15. Experience the joy of freedom from all kinds of karmic lines. Tell yourself:

I am free. I am liberated. I have forgiven myself.
I have forgiven everyone. Everyone has forgiven me.
God of Dusting has forgiven me.
I am experiencing this joy. I am happy. I am happiness.
This joy is pervading the world and cleansing everyone.
The vibrations of this joy are expanding
as far as my field of awareness extends…
far and wide… on the other side of the hills; everywhere.
The white board of pure Consciousness, devoid of bondage,
is awakening universally and shining forth.
Everyone is happy. Everyone is free.
Thank you. Thank you. Thank you.

In this way, spread love, joy and forgiveness to everyone. Help everyone become cleansed from within. God, guru and grace are with you in this endeavor.

16. Tell to God of Dusting:

Dear GoD,
Please continue the task of cleansing and emptying everyone
even after leaving my field of awareness.
Thank you. Thank you. Thank you.

17. Slowly open your eyes.

Seeker A: Thank you for this precious guidance. I am feeling light and serene.

Seeker B: Gratitude to you for this opportunity. There are so many aspects to life and karma that we were unaware of. I realize that we can imbibe this wisdom only through this regular practice.

Sirshree: Listening to this knowledge is a wake-up call for who-you-truly-are. It awakens your true nature and establishes you in the experience of pure Consciousness. Practice forgiveness regularly at every opportunity and let its magic unfold in your life and also of everyone around you. Thank you for this opportunity to serve you. Let life blossom and spread its divine fragrance through all of you!

■ ■ ■

You can mail your opinion or feedback on this book to:
books.feedback@tejgyan.org

About Sirshree

Sirshree's spiritual quest, which began during his childhood, led him on a journey through various schools of philosophy and meditation practices. He studied a wide range of literature on mind science and spirituality. After a long period of deep contemplation on the truth of life, his quest culminated in attaining the ultimate truth.

Sirshree espouses, "All spiritual paths that lead to the truth begin differently but culminate at the same point – Understanding. This understanding is complete in itself. Listening to this understanding is enough to attain the Truth." Over the last two decades, he has dedicated his life to raise mass consciousness.

Sirshree has delivered more than 4000 discourses that throw light on this understanding. He has designed a system for wisdom, which makes it accessible to all. This system has inspired people from all walks of life to progress on their journey of the Truth. Thousands of seekers join in a virtual prayer for World Peace and Global Healing daily at 9:09 am and 9:09 pm.

About Tej Gyan Foundation

Tej Gyan Foundation is a non-profit organization founded on the teachings of Sirshree. The Foundation disseminates Tejgyan – the wisdom that guides one from self-development to Self-realization, leading towards Self-stabilization.

The Foundation's system for imparting wisdom has been assessed by international quality auditors and accredited with the ISO 9001:2015 certification. This wisdom has been presented in a simple, systematic, and practically applicable form that makes it accessible to people from all walks of life, regardless of religion, caste, social strata, country, or belief system.

The Foundation has centers in more than 400 cities and towns across India and other countries. The mission of Tej Gyan Foundation is to create a highly evolved society by leading seekers from negative thoughts to positive thoughts and further, from positive thoughts to Happy thoughts. A 'Happy thought' is the auspicious thought of being free from all thoughts, leading to the state of supreme bliss beyond thoughts.

If you seek such wisdom that leads you beyond mere knowledge, dissolves all problems, frees you from all limiting beliefs, reveals the true nature of divinity, and establishes you in the ultimate truth, then it is time to discover Tejgyan; it is time to rise above the mundane knowledge of words and experience Tejgyan!

The MahaAasmani Magic of Awakening Retreat

Self-development to Self-realization towards Self-stabilization

Do you wish to experience unconditional happiness that is not dependent on any reason? Happiness that is permanent and only increases with time? Do you wish to experience love, peace, self-belief, harmony in relationships, prosperity, and true contentment? Do you wish to progress in all facets of your life, viz. physical, mental, social, financial, and spiritual?

If you seek answers to these questions and are thirsty for the ultimate truth, then you are welcome to participate in the MahaAasmani Magic of Awakening retreat organized by Tej Gyan Foundation. This is the Foundation's flagship retreat based on the teachings of Sirshree.

The purpose of this retreat

The purpose of this retreat is that every human being should:

- Discover the answer to "Who am I" and "Why am I?" through direct experience and be established in ultimate bliss.

- Learn the art of living in the present, free from the burden of the past and the anxiety of the future.

- Acquire practical tools to help quieten the chattering mind and dissolve problems.

- Discover missing links in the practices of Meditation (*Dhyana*), Action (*Karma*), Wisdom (*Gyana*), and Devotion (*Bhakti*).

About Books by Sirshree

Sirshree's published work includes more than 150 book titles, some of which have been translated into more than 10 languages. His literature provides a profound reading on various topics of practical living and unravels the missing links in karma, wisdom, devotion, meditation, and consciousness.

His books have been published by leading publishing houses like Penguin, Hay House, Bloomsbury, Wisdom Tree, Jaico, etc. "The Source" book series, authored by Sirshree, has sold over 10 million copies. Various luminaries and celebrities like His Holiness the Dalai Lama, publishers Mr. Reid Tracy, Ms. Tami Simon and Yoga Master Dr. B. K. S. Iyengar have released Sirshree's books and lauded his work.

The Source
Attain Both, Inner Peace
and Worldly success

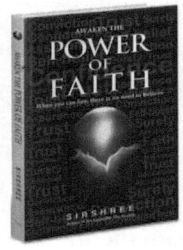

Awaken the Power of Faith
Discover the 7 Principles of the
Highest Power of the Universe

To order books authored by Sirshree, login to:
www.gethappythoughts.org
For further details, call: +91 9011013210

SELECT BOOKS AUTHORED BY SIRSHREE

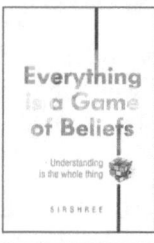   

   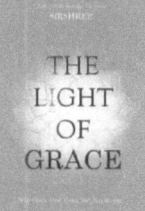

To order these and other books authored by Sirshree
Visit **www.gethappythoughts.org**

Tej Gyan Foundation – Contact details

Registered Office:
Happy Thoughts Building, Vikrant Complex, Near Tapovan Mandir, Pimpri, Pune 411017, INDIA. Contact: +91 20-27411240, +91 20-27412576

MaNaN Ashram:
Survey No. 43, Sanas Nagar, Nandoshi Gaon, Kirkatwadi Phata, Off Sinhagad Road, Taluka Haveli, Pune district - 411024, INDIA. Contact: +91 992100 8060.

WORLD PEACE PRAYER

Divine Light of Love, Bliss, and Peace is Showering;
The Golden Light of Higher Consciousness is Rising;
All negativity on Earth is Dissolving;
Everyone is in Peace and Blissfully Shining;
O God, Gratitude for Everything!

Members of Tej Gyan Foundation have been offering this impersonal mass prayer for many years. Those who are happy can offer this prayer. Those feeling low or suffering from illness can receive healing with this prayer.

If you are feeling troubled or sick, please sit to receive the healing effect of this prayer. Visualize that the divine white healing light is being showered on earth through the prayers of thousands and is also reaching you, bringing you peace and good health. You can dwell in this feeling for some time and then offer your gratitude to those offering the prayer.

A Humble Appeal

More than a million peace lovers pray for World Peace and Global Healing every morning and evening at 9:09. Also, a prayer (in Hindi) to elevate consciousness is webcast every day on YouTube at 3:30 pm and 9:00 pm IST. Please participate in this noble endeavor.

www.ingramcontent.com/pod-product-compliance
Lightning Source LLC
LaVergne TN
LVHW041713070526
838199LV00045B/1325